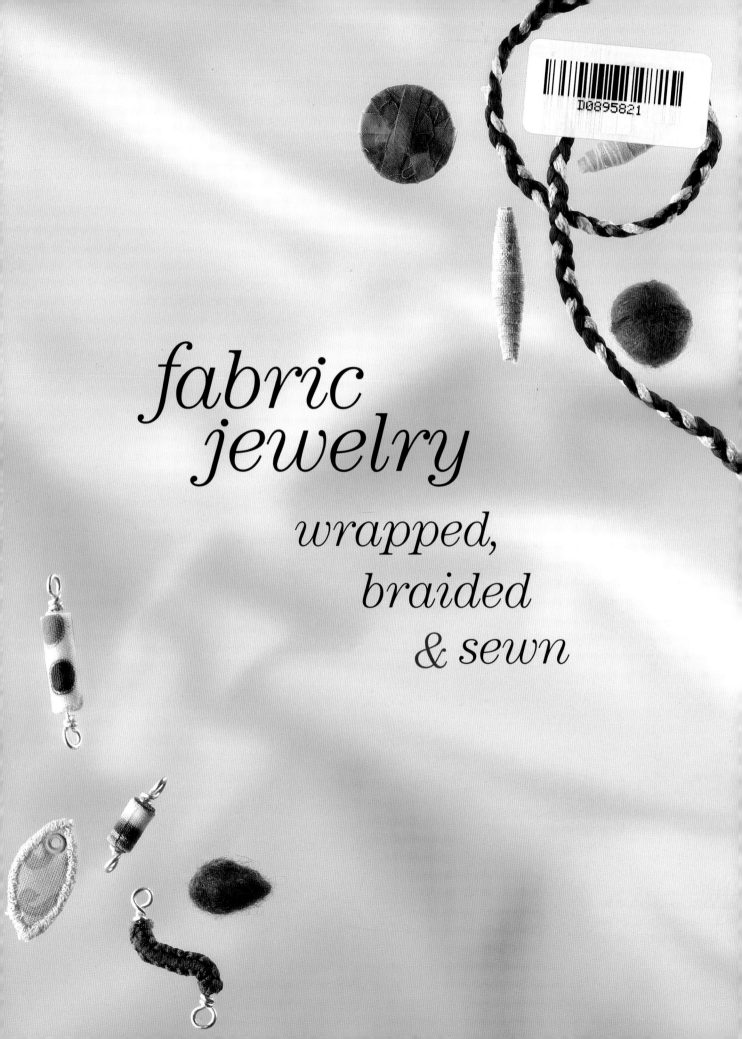

fabric jewelry

wrapped, braided & sewn

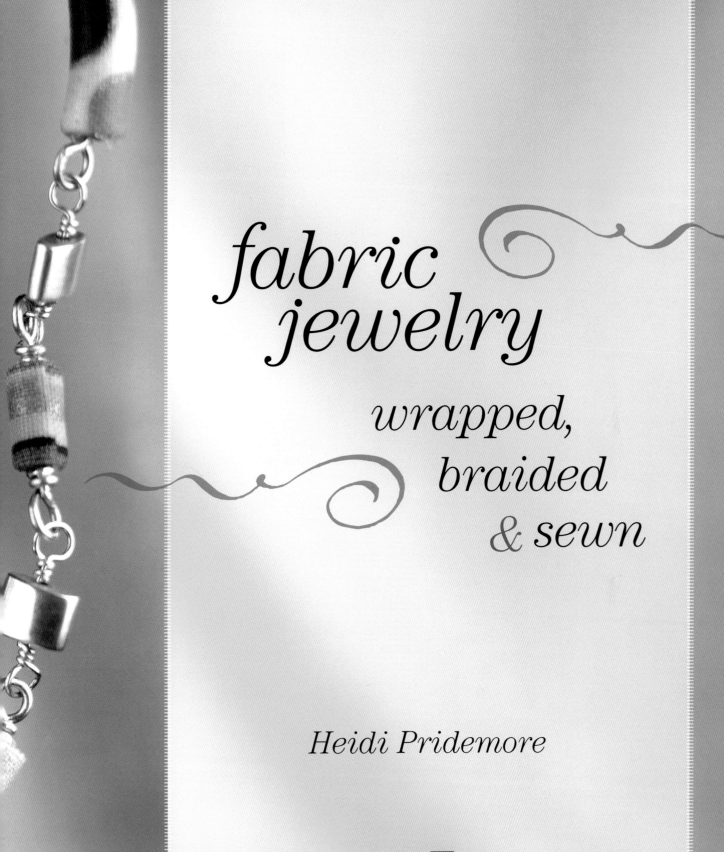

fabric jewelry

wrapped, braided & sewn

Heidi Pridemore

KRAUSE PUBLICATIONS
CINCINNATI, OHIO

www.mycraftivity.com
connect. create. explore.

Fabric Jewelry Wrapped, Braided and Sewn. Copyright © 2009 by Heidi Pridemore and Nancy Zieman. Manufactured in China. All rights reserved. The patterns and drawings in this book are for the personal use of the reader. By permission of the author and publisher, they may be either hand-traced or photocopied to make single copies, but under no circumstances may they be resold or republished. No other part of this book may be reproduced in any form or by any electronic or mechanical means including information storage and retrieval systems without

permission in writing from the publisher, except by a reviewer who may quote brief passages in a review. Published by Krause Publications, an imprint of F+W Media, Inc., 4700 East Galbraith Road, Cincinnati, Ohio, 45236. (800) 289-0963. First Edition.

www.fwmedia.com

13 12 11 10 09   5 4 3 2 1

DISTRIBUTED IN CANADA BY FRASER DIRECT
100 Armstrong Avenue
Georgetown, ON, Canada L7G 5S4
Tel: (905) 877-4411

DISTRIBUTED IN THE U.K. AND EUROPE BY DAVID & CHARLES
Brunel House, Newton Abbot, Devon, TQ12 4PU, England
Tel: (+44) 1626 323200, Fax: (+44) 1626 323319
Email: postmaster@davidandcharles.co.uk

DISTRIBUTED IN AUSTRALIA BY CAPRICORN LINK
P.O. Box 704, S. Windsor NSW, 2756 Australia
Tel: (02) 4577-3555

Library of Congress Cataloging in Publication Data
Pridemore, Heidi
  Fabric jewelry wrapped, braided & sewn / Heidi Pridemore. -- 1st ed.
    p. cm.
  Includes index.
  ISBN 978-1-4402-0250-6 (alk. paper)
  1. Jewelry making. 2. Textile crafts. I. Title.
  TT212.P73 2009
  739.27--dc22
                      2009033472

Editor: *Jennifer Claydon*
Designer: *Julie Barnett*
Production coordinators: *Matt Wagner and Greg Nock*
Photographers: *Christine Polomsky, Ric Deliantoni and Al Parrish*
Stylist: *Lauren Emmerling*

metric conversion chart

TO CONVERT	TO	MULTIPLY BY
inches	centimeters	2.54
centimeters	inches	0.4
feet	centimeters	30.5
centimeters	feet	0.03
yards	meters	0.9
meters	yards	1.1

ABOUT THE AUTHOR

Heidi Pridemore received a bachelor's degree in Industrial Design from Rochester Institute of Technology in 1995. After graduation she worked for several companies in the craft industry as a designer. In 1998 Heidi started her own design studio doing product development for a variety of companies. In 2000 her design studio started to work exclusively with fabric companies around the country, designing quilts and pattern sheets for trade shows and publications. In 2002 she created her own line of quilt patterns and in 2004 Heidi started designing fabric in her own bright and whimsical style. She currently designs fabric for Blank Quilting. Heidi is known for her whimsical, fun quilts which she often makes in dramatic, bright colors. She has designed many quilt patterns for a variety of quilting magazines such as *Quiltmaker*, *McCall's QuickQuilts*, *The Quilter Magazine* and *Quilter's World*. In addition, Heidi is the author of four books: *Quilted Whimsy* (Leisure Arts), *Bold Batik Quilts* (Leisure Arts), *Dazzling Designs* (Leisure Arts) and *Pop-Up Paper Structures* (C&T Publishing). Heidi spends most of her time designing and traveling to trade shows, teaching workshops and giving lectures around the country. When not traveling she spends her time in Arizona with her husband, Matthew, and their dog, Cleo, a Great Pyrenees. Please visit Heidi at her Web site: www.TheWhimsicalWorkshop.com.

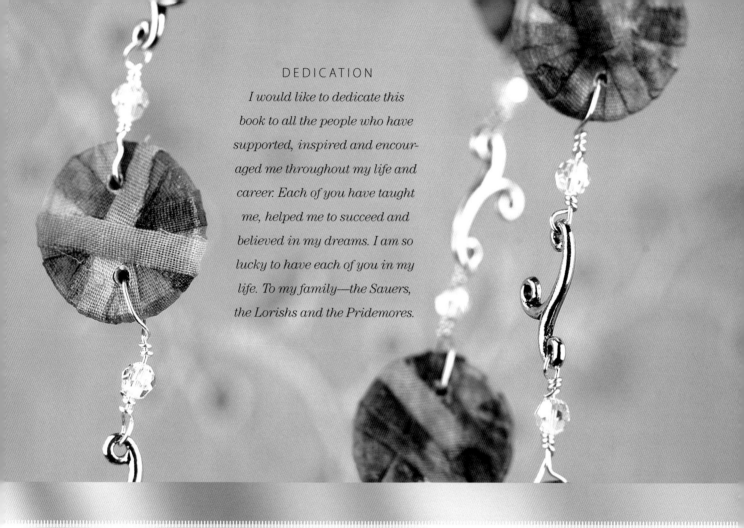

DEDICATION

I would like to dedicate this book to all the people who have supported, inspired and encouraged me throughout my life and career. Each of you have taught me, helped me to succeed and believed in my dreams. I am so lucky to have each of you in my life. To my family—the Sauers, the Lorishs and the Pridemores.

ACKNOWLEDGMENTS

I would like to thank the team at The Whimsical Workshop for all of their hard work and dedication. To my partners, Jerry and Doris Pridemore, without you, I would not be where I am today. Jerry, thank you for all you do to keep things running and for all the support and advice over the years. Doris, you make all our quilts shine with your amazing long-arm quilting and your continued support. I would like to thank Kathy Norton, who has taught me so much and been through so many adventures with me. To many more adventures to come. I would also like to thank Linda Valentino for always working so hard and for keeping us organized and staying cheerful through it all. I know this no small feat. And finally, to Gary Cantwell, our honorary marketing advisor and dear friend. Your encouragement and advice over the years have been priceless. Thanks to each of you for believing in me and working so hard to make The Whimsical Workshop succeed. A special thank you to Matthew, my best friend, soul mate and husband. Thank you for your support and hard work over the years to make my dreams become a reality.

Some other special people I need to mention are Lu Peters, Connie Akers, Mary Kortermeyer and Ann McLaughlin. These amazing women have taught me so much about life and art. Each of you has strongly influenced my work and me. I am so lucky to call you my friends.

To my parents, Douglas and Michael, for encouraging and supporting me through the years. Thank you for all your sacrifices, so I could follow my dreams. To my sisters, Stacey and Echelle, I am so lucky to have you!

Last, but not least, I would like to thank everyone at Krause who worked to make this book a reality. Especially Candy Wiza, Jennifer Claydon and Christine Polomsky for all your hard work. Thank you to Nancy Zieman and everyone at Nancy Zieman Productions for seeing the potential of this project and walking me through the DVD process.

contents

When I first started to quilt, I could not get enough of the beautiful fabrics. The colors and patterns spoke to me in a way no other art medium had. I jumped into quilting and took to it like a duck to water (and if my husband is to be believed, I even talked about quilting in my sleep). I got a part-time job working in a quilt store so I could spend more time with my new fabric friends. I loved pulling different bolts of fabrics from around the store to mix and match them. The fabrics would speak to me and I could easily envision the amazing quilts they would make, if only I had time to sit down and sew. The highlight of working in a quilt store was picking fabrics for the customers' projects because I got to see the fabrics go on to become quilts that I envisioned, but I didn't have to do the work. My passion for quilting and fabrics became the driving force behind my own business.

Mixing two passions to create amazing jewelry

But, as with any hobby that becomes a business, I could no longer look at fabric the way I had before. Fabric became a part of my job as a designer; I still loved fabrics and enjoyed quilting, but I looked at fabrics differently. I would always find myself asking, "Can I use it for an upcoming project," or "Will our customers like this?" This started to affect the way I picked fabrics and the fabrics stopped speaking to me.

As quilting became my business, I had to find a new hobby. Jewelry fit the bill. I was as obsessed with all the beautiful beads I found as I had been with fabric. Beads inspired me the same way fabric had. I could envision finished pieces each time I bought beads. I made jewelry to complement my wardrobe and fit my tastes. Unlike quilting, I was determined to keep jewelry-making my hobby and that idea worked for a couple of years. Then, one day I started to look at the fabrics in my studio while working on jewelry. I started to wonder how I could mix my two passions, fabric and beads, together. I wanted to see if I could create elegant jewelry with both fabrics and beads. As I made my first piece, I realized there was so much I could do by mixing fabrics, beads and findings together. I kept exploring different techniques, sometimes beading techniques alone and sometimes adding quilting and sewing techniques. I was so excited with the results.

Fabrics that had stopped talking to me over the years had a new voice. I was excited to go to a fabric store again and with fabric jewelry I did not need much fabric to create a piece of jewelry. Time was another bonus to making fabric jewelry—most of the projects that follow can be done in a couple of hours, unlike a quilt that can take much longer.

I sat down and considered just what to do with my exciting new discovery. I wondered if anyone else would be as interested in these techniques as I was. When I shared my projects, I was thrilled that others were inspired by the techniques I had used and decided to share them through a book.

When I began this book, I wanted to make sure that people who have never made jewelry and people who have never sewn could make the majority of the projects shown here. So, this is a beginner's guide to making fabric jewelry for everyone, regardless of skill level. These projects are a bridge between fabric lovers and bead lovers because you need both to make these projects. If you love beads, I'll introduce you to the fabulous world of fabric. If you are a fabric fanatic, take a look at jewelry to find a new world of inspiration. And if you're new to both worlds, I hope this will be a wonderful introduction to each one! Who would have guessed that the blending of my passions, beads and fabric, could become elegant and fun jewelry for any occasion?

I am so excited to share my projects with you and encourage you to build on these techniques. Explore mixing these mediums together and see what beautiful results you come up with.

Happy creating!

CHAPTER ONE

Tools and Materials

Fabric jewelry is a combination of jewelry making and fiber crafts that uses a wide range of techniques from both fields. Because of the nature of this craft and the combination of two different mediums, there is a long list of tools and materials in this chapter. Read this chapter before moving on to the projects in the book, then check the projects you want to create to see what materials and tools you will need. You will not need everything listed in this chapter for every project.

One of the most important considerations when making fabric jewelry is the combination of fabrics with other materials and the way they work together. Fabric beads are very light and tend to not hang correctly by themselves. Adding glass, metal or other beads with a bit of weight to them solves this problem. Look for pieces that complement the fabrics and fibers you are using and that will add weight to the the project.

Each type of jewelry has its own unique needs to consider when you are making or designing a piece. Necklaces need to have some weight so they will drape nicely on the neckline. Bracelets need to have durability and the beads need to feel comfortable on your wrist. Earrings need to be carefully balanced—too heavy and the earrings will be uncomfortable, too light and they will not hang correctly. For every type of jewelry, the materials have to feel comfortable next to your skin. Keep these factors in mind and have fun picking your combination of fabrics, findings and beads as you start to make your own fabric jewelry.

Fabric

Most of the projects in this book use high-quality, 100 percent cotton fabric. Quilting cottons and batik fabrics work well because they have a tight weave, and fabrics with a tight weave fray less. You can learn to judge the weave based on touch by comparing fabrics from various fabric companies. Other fabrics that work well with these techniques are silk, rayon and cotton lamé. Fabrics that are a solid color, mottled or have small-scale prints on them are the best to start with because they will yield the most predictable results. Once you understand the basics of making the different fabric beads and how the fabrics interact with each technique, experiment with a variety of fabrics and prints for different looks.

Ribbon

Ribbon can be a wonderful substitute for fabric in beads. Ribbons are already narrow enough to make beads and have finished edges that do not fray. I recommend rayon ribbon to start with because it handles like fabric and drapes nicely. With practice and patience you can use grosgrain ribbon for a textured look or satin ribbon for added elegance. There are also many specialty ribbons available—I recommend testing a small piece before investing in a lot of yardage.

Wool

In Chapter Six, we explore making jewelry with wool in both fabric and roving form. There are many wonderful colors available in wool fabric and roving that can be used to make stunning jewelry. Wool roving is usually used for spinning yarn and is made up of wool fibers that have been combed. The wool fibers have scales that, when rolled with soap and warm water, lock together. You can use this process, called felting, to form beads. A little roving goes a long way, so buy small amounts unless you really love the color. Wool fabric is sold by the yard and I recommend buying fabric that has already been felted. Since fabric beads only use a small amount of wool, a sample book of fabrics, which usually has 5"–6" (13cm–15cm) squares, is a great way to go. These pieces are large enough to make beads from.

Cords and Threads

A variety of threads and cords are used throughout this book both for construction and as decorative elements. There are many other cords, yarns and threads available besides the ones listed here—try them out, as you might like the results. The following cords and threads are used in this book.

Beading thread comes in a wide variety of colors and is made from synthetic materials such as polyethylene or nylon. These threads are strong, but can stretch over time unless you condition them. To condition the thread, stretch the piece of thread and slide it through beeswax or another thread conditioner. I recommend using beading thread that matches the colors in your project to help the thread "disappear" in the project.

Sewing machine thread is used for projects that are made using a sewing machine. For a satin-stitched edge, I recommend using 40 weight rayon thread made for machine embroidery. This type of thread comes in many colors and has a wonderful finish once stitched.

Embroidery floss and pearl cotton are perfect for thread-wrapped projects like those in Chapter Four. Again, I recommend using rayon embroidery threads because rayon creates such an elegant finished piece.

Cords and yarns have a variety of uses in fabric jewelry and there are many different varieties available in knitting and needlepoint stores. I recommend cords and yarns that have a smooth finish so your beads do not have little hairs sticking out everywhere. This is a personal preference, though, and I encourage you to try out different yarns and cords. The sky's the limit here, just make sure you like the feel of the fiber against your skin. There is nothing quite like an itchy necklace or bracelet to make you crazy.

Bead Cores

Several types of beads can be created by wrapping fabric and threads around a core. Once you have tried your hand at the projects in this book, look around and see what other found objects might work. The core needs to either already have a hole for stringing, or needs to be made from a material that you can drill or punch a hole through. The following items are used as bead cores in the projects in this book.

Wood shapes can be bought at woodworking or craft stores. If you are handy with a jigsaw, you can create your own shapes from a thin piece of wood.

Metal washers are great for creating donut-shaped beads. They come in an assortment of sizes and can be bought at any hardware store. While you are there, check out other pieces of hardware that can be wrapped.

Buttons make wonderful bead cores. Shank buttons work best for wrapped techniques, but a standard button can also be wrapped, as long as you can poke through the wrapping fabric to reach the buttonhole.

Heavy-weight stabilizer can be folded and sewn along with fabric to create beautiful beads. This product can be found at fabric or quilting stores.

Coating Gels

Most of the beads in this book are coated as the final step to give the beads a shiny finish while leaving them soft enough to sew through. I found that acrylic mediums (made for use with acrylic paints to build texture) work wonderfully to finish the beads. One of the best things about these products is that most of them are nontoxic. You can find these products at most art stores alongside the acrylic paints. I recommend using the Golden or Liquitex brands due to their quality.

Acrylic glazing liquid is a liquid medium designed to help acrylic paints have a longer working time. I like to use these products as the first coat on any of the fabric beads. It is very easy to work with and has some tack to it, which helps hold the piece together as you work. Acrylic glazing liquids are available in satin or gloss finish. This product can also be used as the final finish—add several coats, letting each coat dry before applying the next.

Heavy gel makes the perfect topcoat when you want to have a thick, glossy coat that does not change the color of the fabrics in the bead. Use heavy gel on beads that have a smooth surface.

Self-leveling gel is also a wonderful topcoat to use for a glossy coat that does not change the color of the fabric. Self-leveling gel can smooth out a slightly uneven surface because it will fill in small spaces created by gaps in the fabrics or threads.

Clear tar gel is thicker than the other gels listed here. It is great if you want to build up a texture or want to cover dimensional features and maintain the dimension. Clear tar gel will make the fabrics look darker and will leave a shiny finish.

Adhesives

There are several adhesives used throughout this book and I have selected each of them because of how they work for different materials. Use the best adhesives you can buy because the glue is what holds everything together. Experiment with adhesives before using them in a project. The adhesives you choose should dry clear and should also be waterproof because the piece will likely get wet at some time during the course of normal wear.

Jeweler's cement is available at most jewelry supply stores. I prefer G-S Hypo Cement and I use it to secure all of the knots in a project. It also works well for gluing beads onto a cord or chain. It sets up quickly and cleans up easily.

Industrial strength craft adhesives such as E-6000 work well for a permanent bond. I like to use this type of adhesive when I glue terminators in place on my pieces. This adhesive works well on wood, glass, plastic, metal, fibers and much more, which makes it very versatile.

Fabric glue is used to adhere fabrics and fibers. Many different brands are available—use the one that works best for you. I apply fabric glue with an old paintbrush to make a thin, even layer. If you are working with glue that dries quickly, work in small sections across the fabric.

Paper-backed fusible web is made from a fiber that melts when heat is applied. When fusible web is placed between two layers of fabric and ironed, the melting fibers adhere the two pieces of fabric. Fusible web comes in sheets or on a roll and is available at most quilting and craft stores. Fusible web can also adhere fabric to wood or cardboard, as well as other materials. There are many brands of fusible web available; experiment with different brands to decide which works the best for you. If you get fusible web on your iron, use an iron cleaner such as Iron-Off to clean the iron before using the iron on fabric. If you are in a pinch, try using a fabric softener sheet to clean the bottom of the iron.

Liquid seam sealant is used to keep the raw edges of fabrics and ribbon from fraying by sealing the loose threads in place. I prefer to use Fray Check—it does not discolor or stain most fabrics. However, it is always smart to test it on a piece of scrap fabric first. Apply seam sealant to the raw edges or exposed corners of fabric or ribbon on any of the projects in this book to keep the piece from fraying.

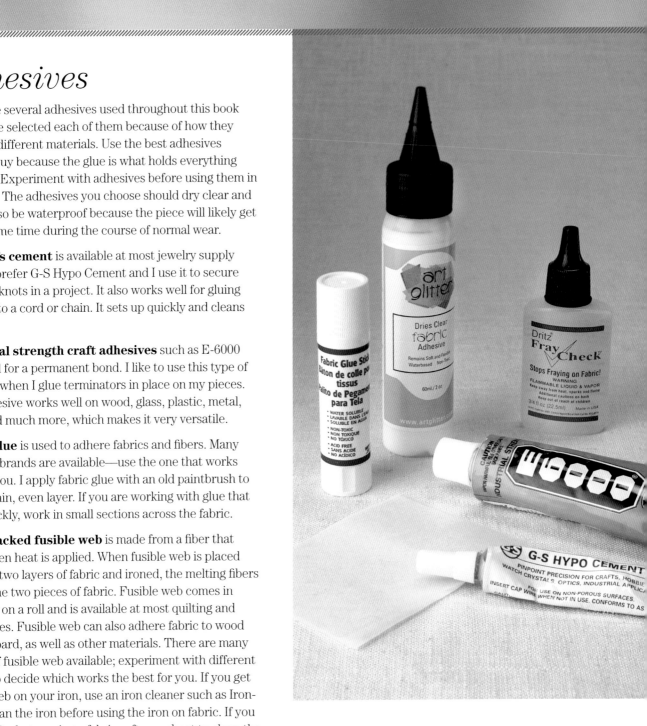

Beads

Glass, metal, wood, crystal and stone beads can all be mixed into each project for weight. Fabric and fiber beads are very light-weight and tend to not hang well by themselves, but by mixing other types of beads with the fabric beads, you can give a project the heft it needs, as well as complement and enhance the appearance of the fabric beads. The following types of beads work well in fabric jewelry projects.

Seed beads are very small glass beads that come in a variety of sizes; the sizes are denoted by a number that represents how many beads fit side by side in 1" (3cm). Seed beads come in different shapes—rounds, triangles and squares are just a few. Seed beads also come in many different colors and finishes, so it is easy to find the right bead for the job.

Bugle beads are small, cylindrical beads about the same diameter as seed beads, but longer. These are great to use as a spacer or filler bead. Bugle beads tend to have sharp edges that over time can wear through stringing threads. I use doubled threads with bugle beads for added security.

Focus beads become the center of a project and all of the other beads in the project are selected to match the centerpiece. This bead is usually larger than the rest. I like to collect unique focus beads when I find them and I keep a whole stash of different beads for future projects.

Accent beads are used to enhance a design; they're smaller than the focus bead but larger than seed beads. I like to select glass, crystal and metal beads for accents in my projects. I recommend purchasing at least eight beads for a bracelet or twelve beads for a necklace. It is always better to have a few extra than not enough.

Spacer beads are used in between accent beads and focus beads and usually have a disk shape. I like to collect attractive spacer beads when I find them so I can keep them on hand for future projects. I recommend buying fifteen to twenty beads for a necklace and ten to fifteen beads for a bracelet.

Findings

Jewelry findings are used to construct a piece of jewelry. I have listed the findings used in this book below with a brief description of each one. Knowing what each finding is used for can be helpful when planning your own pieces of jewelry.

Crimp beads are used to add clasps to the end of beading wire or to secure a bead on the beading wire. Crimp beads come in several sizes; select the crimp bead that fits snugly over two pieces of the beading wire you have selected. The sizes of crimp beads used most often in this book are 2mm and 3mm. Always pick crimp beads that match the metal used throughout the project.

Flexible beading wire is available in many different diameters and finishes. The weight of the beads in the project determines the proper diameter of beading wire for the project. All the projects in this book can be strung on light- or medium-weight beading wire. Experiment with the different brands of wire to find out which one you prefer to work with.

Wire can be bent and formed into different shapes using a few simple tools. Wire is made with a wide assortment of metals and is available in different gauges; the higher the gauge number, the thinner the wire. For smaller beads I like to use 22-gauge wire; for larger beads, I choose 18-gauge wire. When purchasing wire, you also need to choose the hardness of the wire (also known as the temper or malleability of the wire). I like to work with dead soft or half-hard wire because they are easy to bend by hand.

Jump rings are used to attach jewelry elements, including beads, charms and chains. Jump rings come in assorted sizes; it's best to pick the smallest jump ring to do the job. Match the metal in the jump rings to the other metal items used in the project.

Head pins are pieces of wire with one end formed into a stopper, either plain or decorative. You can thread beads onto a head pin to create a dangle on a piece of jewelry. Head pins come in many different lengths and metals. I recommend using longer head pins because they are easier to handle and can be cut down if needed.

Eye pins are pieces of wire with one end formed into a loop. Eye pins are used to form connections to other elements in the piece of jewelry. Like head pins, I prefer to use long eye pins because they are easier to maneuver and join.

Terminators are used at the end of a cord or chain to cover any knots or closures. Terminators can be plain so that they don't attract attention or they can be fancy to add to the overall design of the piece. Some terminators slide over the wire and can be glued in place using a strong adhesive. Others have a crimp section that can be squeezed tightly over the cords using a pair of pliers to keep them from slipping.

Clasps are used to close a necklace or bracelet, and range from utilitarian spring clasps to pieces so ornate that you want to use the clasp in the front of a necklace to show it off. Like other findings, match the clasp metal to the metal used throughout the project.

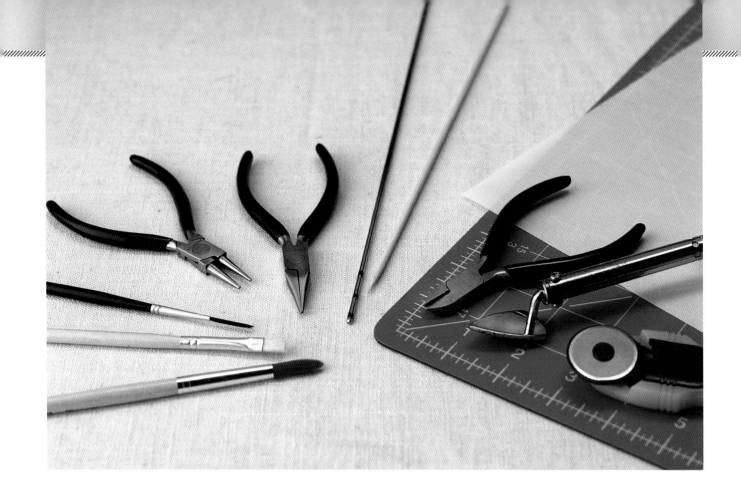

Tools

The projects in this book are made using several different techniques and a variety of jewelry-making and quilting tools. Check the materials list of each project for special tools used only in that project.

Pliers are used to hold, shape and manipulate findings in a piece of jewelry. I recommend jewelry-grade pliers that will not scratch metal findings. Needle-nose pliers (also known as chain-nose pliers) have flat jaws and are the basic pliers used for most jewelry techniques. You will also need round-nose pliers to make round loops with wire; these pliers have round jaws that taper to a point. Crimp pliers are special pliers that are used to close crimp beads and create a professional, finished look. These pliers are optional because crimp beads can also be closed using needle-nose pliers, but the crimp bead will not have the same neat appearance.

Flush cut wire cutters are used to cut or trim wires, head pins and eye pins. Wire cutters will dull over time and you can either have them sharpened or replace them as needed.

Mandrels are used for rolling beads. These metal dowels are usually used to make lampwork beads and can be bought from any glassworks supply store. Bamboo skewers make a good substitute for mandrels. I recommend lightly sanding the skewer before starting to remove any loose slivers of wood.

Paintbrushes are perfect for applying acrylic mediums, adhesives and decorative elements to your fabric beads. A variety of small brushes is all you'll need for jewelry work.

A rotary cutter, acrylic ruler and cutting mat are used to cut fabric. These tools make it easy to get a straight edge when cutting through layers of fabric. I recommend using a 45mm rotary cutter for most projects, but an 18mm rotary cutter can be useful for small pieces. It is important to use a proper cutting mat with a rotary cutter so that the blade stays sharp and the cutter doesn't damage your cutting surface. Any self-healing mat will work with a rotary cutter.

A Teflon pressing sheet is wonderful to work on when using fusible web. The Teflon coating on the sheet keeps fusible web from sticking to the pressing surface or the iron. These are available at most craft and quilting stores.

A mini iron is invaluable to fabric jewelry techniques; due to the size and scale of the beads, it is easier to use a mini iron than a full size one. Mini irons are adjustable and work well with the detail work involved in making fabric jewelry.

A beading mat is made from a piece of textured fabric that keeps the beads from rolling around on your work surface. I like to use a plastic serving tray lined with a beading mat when working to keep everything contained.

An awl is a long metal tool that tapers to a point. It is great for poking holes in fabric beads or to hold tiny pieces in place as you work on them.

Tapestry needles are designed for use with thicker flosses, such as embroidery floss or pearl cotton. These needles are also great to use with ribbons and smaller cords. I recommend a size 22 or size 20 tapestry needle.

Straw needles are long, thin needles usually used in quilting. I prefer to use these to standard beading needles because they are stiffer and do not easily bend when working with them. Straw needles come in a variety of sizes. The larger the number on the needle, the smaller the needle size. Straw needles can be found at quilting and sewing shops. If you cannot find straw needles, try standard sewing needles.

Collapsible eye needles are perfect for stringing beads with very small holes. The eye of the needle is very flexible and can squeeze flat through a bead hole. You can find these needles in most jewelry or craft supply stores.

Felting needles are actually not needles, but thin pieces of barbed metal. Felting needles are used to push wool roving fibers into another piece of wool or fabric to felt the two together. You can find these needles anywhere felting supplies are sold.

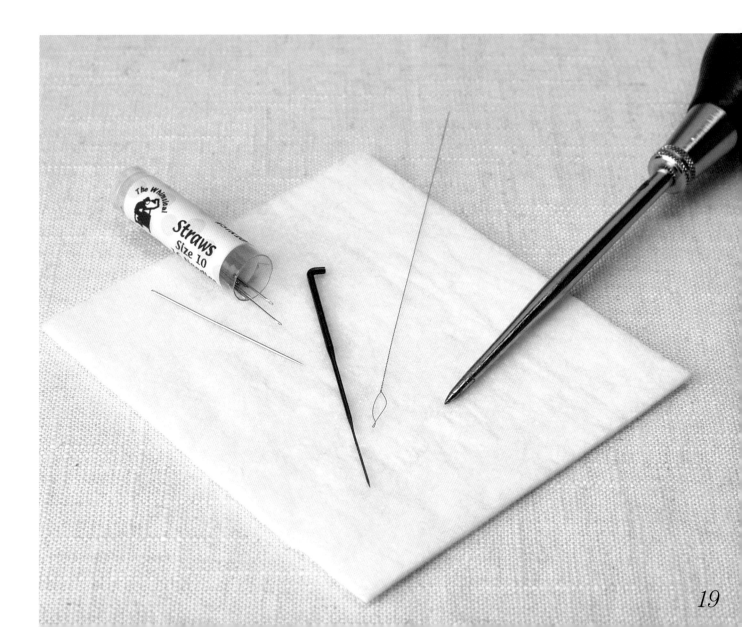

CHAPTER TWO

Basic Techniques

This chapter covers all of the basic techniques used to create the projects in the following chapters. It is important to understand each technique so you can make a piece of jewelry that looks nice and is functional. Jewelry has to hold up to the wear and tear of day-to-day use. It has to be water resistant, if not waterproof. It also has to look good over time and not look worn out after one or two wearings. These are important factors when designing or making a piece of jewelry. Pick materials for your projects that are durable as well as beautiful. Most importantly, understand and practice good construction techniques.

The techniques shown here include construction tips to keep things held together. It is important to know when and how to use these techniques, whether you are creating a project from this book or designing your own masterpiece. If you use good construction techniques in your jewelry, it will last for a very long time and still look good.

In addition to reading this chapter, I also recommend checking out some of the amazing books available on basic jewelry making techniques to expand on the lessons listed in this book. Once you understand how jewelry is made, it is much easier to successfully design your own creations.

Using Crimp Beads

Use crimping pliers with crimp beads to create a finished, professional look. If you prefer, crimp beads can also be closed with needle-nose pliers and still look nice.

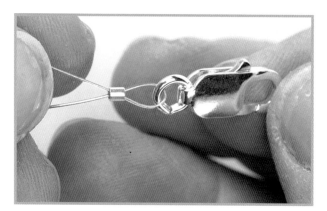

1 **Arrange pieces**

To attach a clasp, slide a crimp bead onto the beading wire and about 2" (5cm) from the end of the wire. Slide the clasp onto the wire, then loop the beading wire back through the crimp bead. Slide the crimp bead up the doubled wire as close to the clasp as you can, then loosen up the crimp slightly to leave a small gap between the clasp and the crimp bead.

2 **Crimp**

To use crimping pliers, first press the crimp bead flat using the hole on the pliers closest to the handle. Holding the wires apart, squeeze the pliers to compress the crimp bead. Make sure there is a wire on each side of the indent. Put the flattened crimp bead on its side in the front hole of the tool with the indent facing the front of the pliers. Press the pliers to fold the crimp bead in half to form a cylinder. Tug on the ends of the wires to make sure everything is secure. If not, place the crimp bead back in the first hole and squeeze a second time.

If you are not using crimping pliers, simply press the crimp bead flat with needle-nose pliers.

Opening and Closing Jump Rings

Jump rings need to be opened and closed a certain way; this will keep the shape of the ring and will allow the ring to close all the way. Follow these steps every time for perfect jump rings.

1 **Grasp ring**

Grasp the jump ring with two pairs of pliers, a pair on each side of the cut in the ring. I use round-nose and needle-nose pliers for this step.

2 **Rotate pliers**

Twist the pliers gently in opposite directions to open the jump ring. You will twist in the opposite direction to close the jump ring. If you have a small gap in your jump ring, gently squeeze the two ends with the needle-nose pliers. In most cases this can close small gaps. If you know how to use a soldering iron, you can also solder the jump rings closed.

Wire Wrapping

Throughout the book I use sterling silver wire as the base for different beads and dangles. To take a straight piece of wire and make it into a piece that can be connected to other elements, you need to create a wire wrap at the end of the wire. When using head pins, you can make a wire-wrapped loop at the top of the head pin to attach it to a chain. The following steps will set you on your way.

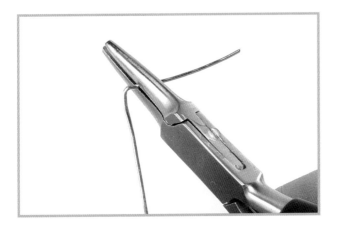

1 Prepare wire

You will need 1" (3cm) of wire for each loop. So, if you want to make a 1" (3cm) bead with a loop at each end, you will need a 3" (8cm) piece of wire—1" (3cm) for each loop and 1" (3cm) for the bead. Make a mark 1" (3cm) from each end of the wire with a permanent marker. Grasp the wire at a 1" (3cm) mark with a pair of needle-nose pliers. Bend the wire at a right angle, flush with the jaws of the pliers.

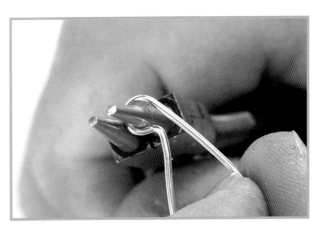

2 Begin loop

Grasp the wire at the bend with round-nose pliers. With your fingers or needle-nose pliers, wrap the wire tail around the right half of the round-nose pliers to begin the loop.

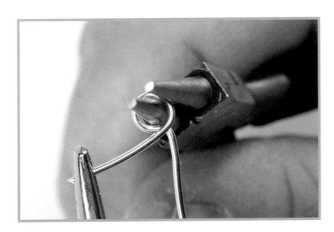

3 Finish loop

Slide the right half of the round-nose pliers out of the loop and slide the loop onto the left half of the pliers. Using the needle-nose pliers, continue to wrap the wire around the round-nose pliers to complete the loop.

If you are going to link the wire onto a chain or other element, slide it onto the loop before the next step.

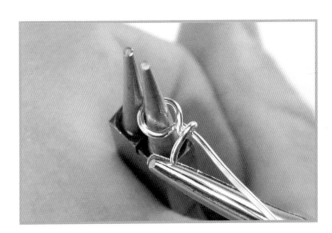

4 Complete wire wrap

Continue to hold the loop with the round-nose pliers while using the needle-nose pliers to wrap the wire tail around the wire under the formed loop. Wrap the tail around at least twice and then trim any excess wire with wire cutters.

Using a Stop Bead

A stop bead is strung onto a thread or cord temporarily to keep the beads in the project from sliding off as you work. A size 8/0 seed bead works great as a stop bead. Once the project is secure, the stop bead is removed.

1 **Begin knot**
Slide a seed bead onto the beading thread or cord. Slide the bead down to the end of the thread leaving a 3" (8cm) tail.

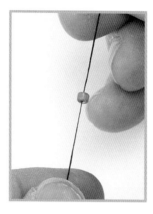

2 **Finish knot**
Thread the beading thread or cord back through the bead again in the same direction so that it wraps around the bead in a loop. The seed bead won't be totally locked in place; it will be able to slide on the cord a bit, but it will keep other beads from sliding off the end.

Tying a Tailor's Knot

A tailor's knot is used in hand sewing. This cool knot works every time and is the perfect knot to use at the start of a project. The size of the knot will be determined by the number of wraps you use around the needle.

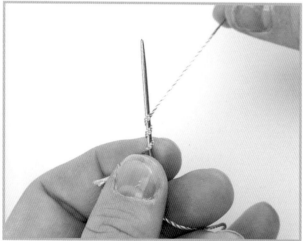

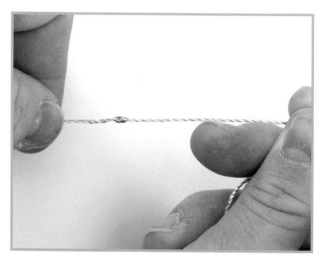

1 **Begin knot**
Thread a needle with the beading thread or cord. Hold the needle with the point of the needle facing up. Take the tail of the thread and wrap it around the needle at least two times.

2 **Finish knot**
Hold the wrapped thread with your thumb and pull the needle up and through. Continue to pull the beading thread or cord through the wraps until the knot is tight at the end. I recommend leaving a tail at least 3" (8cm) long when making jewelry so you can sew the tail into the project before trimming.

Tying an Overhand Knot

An overhand knot is a very simple knot that you probably already know. It is quite handy, and it's used at the end of several projects.

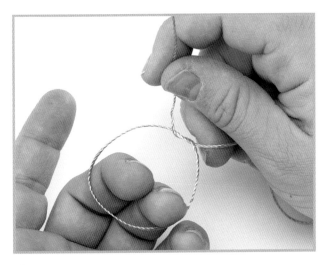

1 Begin knot

Cross the right end of the thread over the left end of the thread, then pull it through the loop.

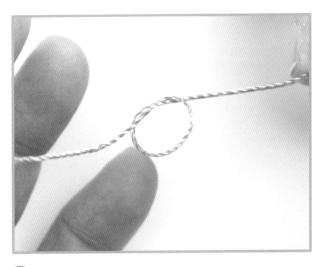

2 Finish knot

Pull on each end of the thread to tighten the knot.

3 Position knot (optional)

If you want the knot to fall in a certain place on the project, you can use an awl or toothpick to position the knot on the cord. Slide the awl into the loop formed by the start of the knot. Pull the knot snug to the tip of the awl. Use the awl to "push" the knot in place. Once the knot is in the desired position, pull the awl out of the loop and finish pulling the knot snug.

Tying a Surgeon's Knot

No matter how well you plan a project using beading thread, sometimes the thread will come up short and you will have to add a new thread to the project to continue. A surgeon's knot is used to add new thread after you tie off the first thread and sew in the tail.

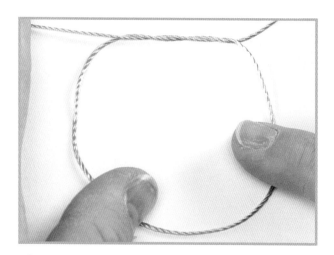

1 Begin knot

Cross the left end of the thread over the right end of the thread and pull it through the loop. Repeat so that the threads are wrapped around each other twice. Pull on each end of the thread to tighten the knot.

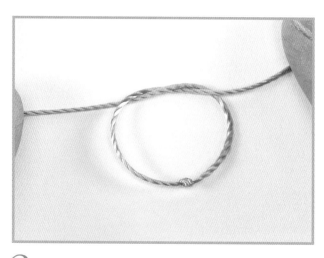

2 Continue knot

Cross the right end of the thread over the left end of the thread, then pull it through the loop.

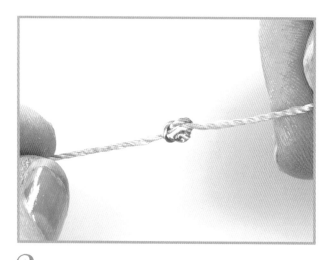

3 Finish knot

Pull on each end of the thread to tighten the second portion of the knot over the first portion.

TIP

When you are adding thread to an ongoing project, start the new thread several beads before the first thread ends. Once you have tied the knot, add a drop of glue to the knot and let it dry completely. Sew the new thread through the beads and bring it out where the first thread stopped.

TIP

There is nothing more disappointing than making a stunning piece of jewelry and the first time it is worn, it falls apart. Knots in jewelry projects can become weak spots if they are not secured. An easy way to secure any knot in your jewelry is to add a drop of jeweler's cement to the center of the knot. It is a small step that can make all the difference in the life of the piece.

Once you have tied a knot, use glue with a syringe tip and slide the syringe tip into the center of the knot. Squeeze a drop of glue in the center of the knot and pull the syringe tip out. Pull the knot snug a second time and let the glue dry completely.

Tying a Half-Hitch Knot

A half-hitch knot is a quick and easy way to attach a pendant or other design element. I find it especially useful with disks and donut beads.

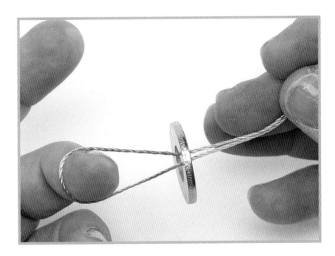

1 **Begin knot**

Fold the thread or cord in half. Slide the loop formed by the cord through the disk.

2 **Finish knot**

Pull the two tail ends through the loop formed around the disk and pull the cord snug.

Burying a Knot

When you are creating fabric beads from layers of fabric, you can hide the starting and ending knots by burying them in the layers of the piece. This quick and easy technique hides the unsightly knot but does not compromise the strength of the knot.

1 Begin burying knot

Decide where you want the thread to start on the piece. Push the threaded needle through a spot on the piece away from the starting point, then pull the needle out at the desired starting point.

2 Finish burying knot

Continue to gently pull the thread until the knot pulls through the outer layer into the interior layers of the piece—the knot should not pull all the way through, but should remain buried between the layers; trim any excess tail that is still showing.

Sewing in Tails

Another finishing technique is sewing the tails of the threads or cords back into the finished piece. A tail helps keep the knot secure, and if you trim the tail flush with a knot, it will eventually come untied. By sewing in the tails you are creating better knots that will not come undone over time.

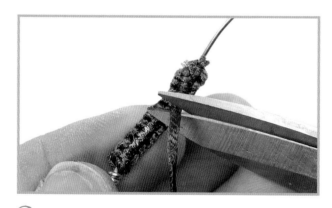

1 Begin sewing

Once the piece is finished, thread each tail onto the needle used for the project, or the smallest needle that will accommodate the thread or cord. Push the needle through the finished piece, usually on the backside if the piece has a front or back.

2 Finish sewing

Pull the needle all the way through and trim any excess end tails that are showing.

CHAPTER THREE

Rocking and Rolling

Rolled beads are the easiest fabric beads to make, but are still quite elegant when mixed with an assortment of glass beads and metal findings. You can create a wide variety of beads by changing the fabric you use, the width of the fabric strips or the finishing glaze. You will only see a small amount of the fabric in each bead, so fabrics with a small print or stripe are great choices for this type of bead. Mottled fabrics and fabrics with metallic finishes are also complementary to this style of bead and create a different look. Whatever fabric you choose, I recommend experimenting with different design elements such as fabric choice and bead finish before you begin a project.

One of the first design choices you need to make is the size of your beads. The length of the fabric strip determines how thick the finished bead will be, while the width of the fabric strip determines the width of the finished bead. The thickness of the mandrel or rod used to roll the bead dictates the diameter of the bead hole. Changing any one of these factors will change the bead's look, so play around to see what combination you like for each set of beads.

The creativity doesn't end once the bead is rolled, either—experiment with finishing the beads, too. You can use acrylic paint to add to your beads like the **Lots-a-Dots Necklace** on page 34. For an added sparkle, mix glitter into acrylic medium before sealing a bead like the **Blue Moon Ladder Bracelet** on page 38. Use the techniques shown here or experiment with other mediums to create your own unique topcoats for your rolled beads.

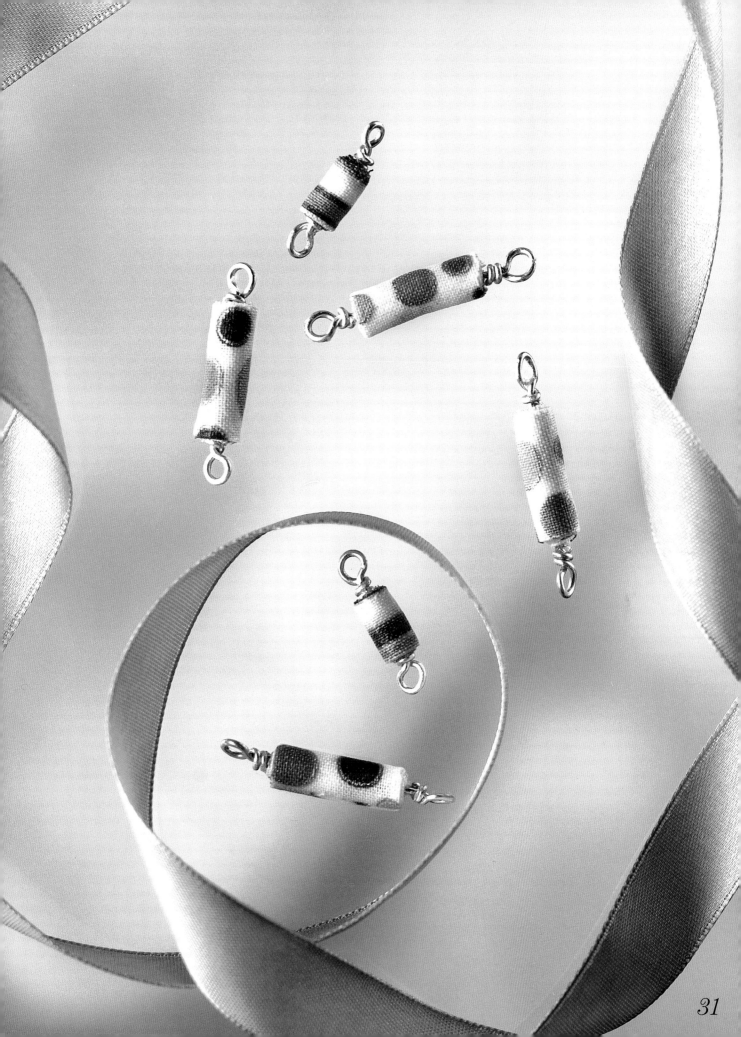

materials

¾" × 5" (2cm × 13cm) fabric strip (for each bead)

Mandrel or bamboo skewer

Paintbrush

Gloss acrylic glazing liquid

Heavy gel

Small pair of scissors, if needed

TIP

Carefully twist the dried beads on the mandrel to loosen them up. Twist the bead and pull upward at the same time to remove the beads from the mandrel. If you pull straight up, you could pull the center fabric out of the bead.

Fabric Barrel Beads

A barrel bead is the easiest rolled bead to create. You may already be familiar with barrel beads—do you remember making them in camp or art school? Because of their simplicity, barrel beads are a great place to start your fabric jewelry adventure.

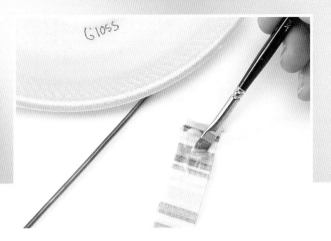

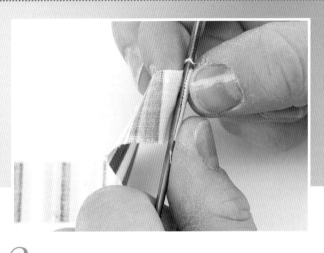

1 Apply acrylic glazing liquid

Paint a thin layer of acrylic glazing liquid on the first 1"–2" (3cm–5cm) of the back of the fabric strip.

2 Begin rolling

Tuck the coated end of the fabric strip tightly to the mandrel. Carefully start to roll the fabric strip around the mandrel.

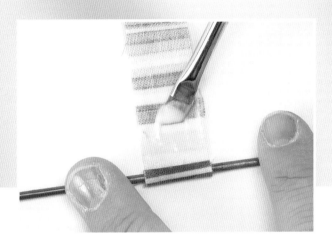

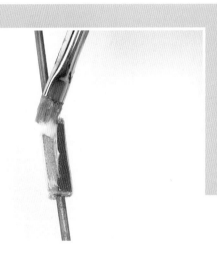

3 Continue rolling

Continue to roll the fabric strip until you reach the portion of the fabric strip not coated with glazing liquid. Brush glazing liquid onto the uncoated portion of the fabric strip and continue to roll until the strip is completely wrapped around the mandrel.

4 Finish bead

Brush another coat of glazing liquid on the finished bead. Let the bead dry completely. Add a second coat of glazing liquid to the bead and let it dry as well. Add 2–3 coats of the heavy gel to the rolled bead. Let each coat dry before applying the next coat.

Remove the dry bead from the mandrel and trim any frayed threads from the edges of the bead.

Heidi has a unique way to dry barrel beads, using an inverted aluminum pan and floral foam! When you watch the DVD, you'll see her ingenious set-up.

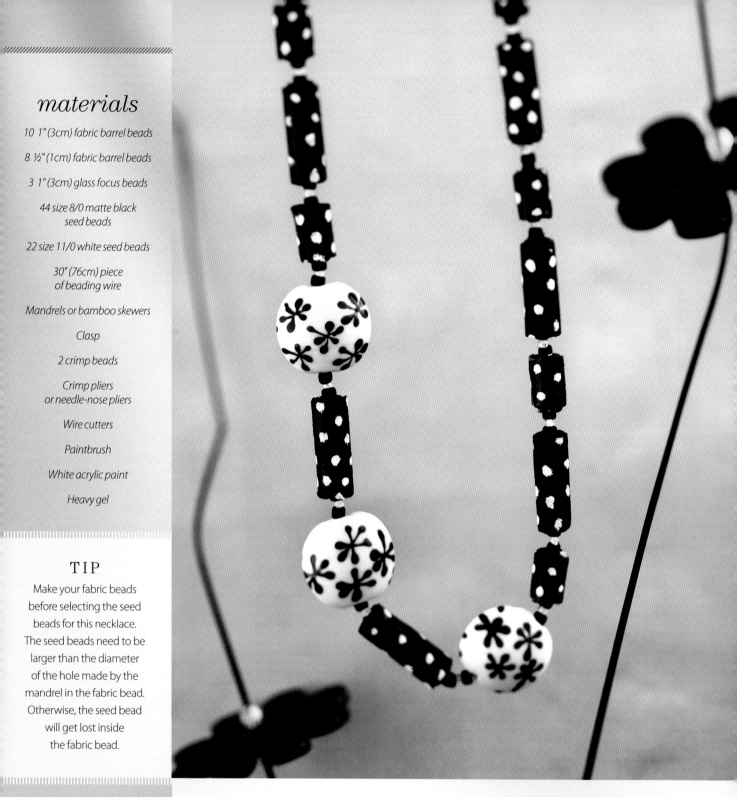

materials

10 1" (3cm) fabric barrel beads

8 ½" (1cm) fabric barrel beads

3 1" (3cm) glass focus beads

44 size 8/0 matte black seed beads

22 size 11/0 white seed beads

30" (76cm) piece of beading wire

Mandrels or bamboo skewers

Clasp

2 crimp beads

Crimp pliers or needle-nose pliers

Wire cutters

Paintbrush

White acrylic paint

Heavy gel

TIP

Make your fabric beads before selecting the seed beads for this necklace. The seed beads need to be larger than the diameter of the hole made by the mandrel in the fabric bead. Otherwise, the seed bead will get lost inside the fabric bead.

Lots-a-Dots Necklace

I wanted to show how easy it is to embellish fabric beads with acrylic paint, and I thought polka dots would be the perfect accent to this piece. Adding accents with paint can change the look of any fabric bead without changing the feel of the finished beads. This is a playful, yet sophisticated, necklace that can add zip to any outfit for a night out on the town.

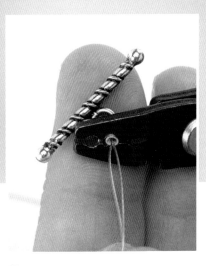

1 Decorate beads

Follow the instructions on pages 32–33 to make 10 1" (3cm) and 8 ½"(1cm) barrel beads. Leave the beads on the mandrels. Use white acrylic paint and a small paintbrush to paint white dots onto the barrel beads. Space the dots evenly over the surface. Let the paint dry. Add another coat of heavy gel to each bead. Let the gel dry and remove the beads from the mandrels.

2 Attach clasp

Slide a crimp bead onto the piece of beading wire about 4" (10cm) from one end. Slide a piece of the clasp onto the beading wire and loop the wire through the crimp bead a second time. Use the crimp pliers or needle-nose pliers to close the crimp bead in place (see *Using Crimp Beads*, page 22).

3 Begin stringing

String the beads onto the beading wire in the following sequence: 8/0 black seed bead, 11/0 white seed bead, 8/0 black seed bead (abbreviated in this pattern as Blk/Wht/Blk combo), 1" (3cm) fabric bead, Blk/Wht/Blk combo, ½" (1cm) fabric dot bead. Repeat the beading pattern 3 more times.

4 Complete necklace

To make the focus section of the necklace, string the beads onto the wire in the following sequence: Blk/Wht/Blk combo, 1" (3cm) glass focus bead, Blk/Wht/

Blk combo, 1" (3cm) fabric dot bead, Blk/Wht/Blk combo, 1" (3cm) glass focus bead, Blk/Wht/Blk combo, 1" (3cm) fabric dot bead, Blk/Wht/Blk combo, 1" (3cm) glass focus bead, Blk/Wht/Blk combo.

To finish stringing the necklace, string the beads onto the wire in the following sequence: ½" (1cm) fabric dot bead, Blk/Wht/Blk combo, 1" (3cm) fabric dot bead, Blk/Wht/Blk combo. Repeat the beading pattern 3 more times.

Slide the remaining crimp bead onto the beading wire. Slide the other half of the clasp onto the wire and loop the wire back through the crimp bead. Use crimp pliers or needle-nose pliers to close the crimp bead in place. Thread the extra wire at each end through the first few beads for added strength. Trim the excess wire with wire cutters.

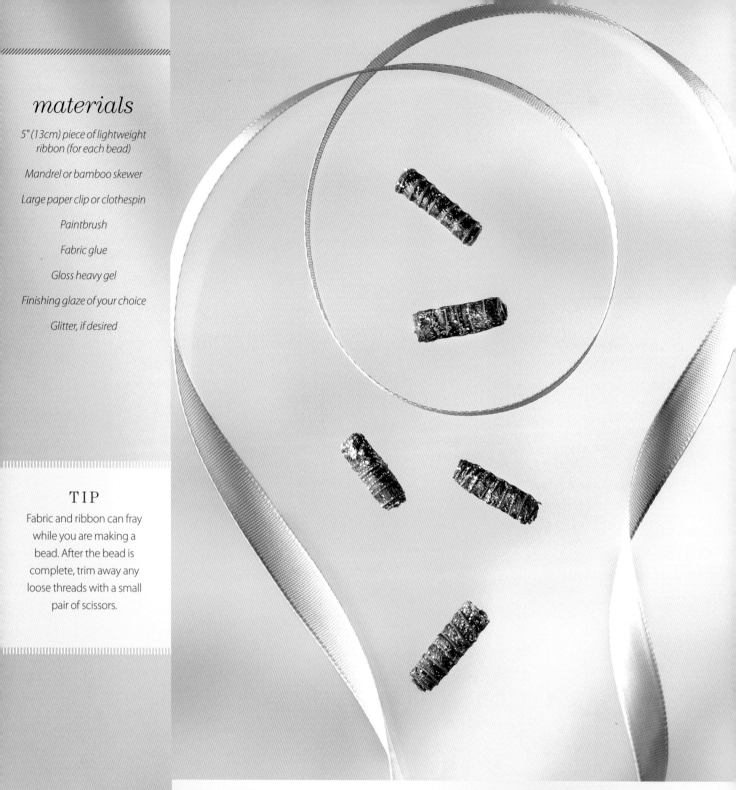

materials

5" (13cm) piece of lightweight ribbon (for each bead)

Mandrel or bamboo skewer

Large paper clip or clothespin

Paintbrush

Fabric glue

Gloss heavy gel

Finishing glaze of your choice

Glitter, if desired

TIP

Fabric and ribbon can fray while you are making a bead. After the bead is complete, trim away any loose threads with a small pair of scissors.

Ribbon Barrel Beads

Barrel beads can also be made with beautiful ribbons, although they may require some special handling. Lightweight ribbons are the same to work with as fabric when making barrel beads. Medium-weight ribbons and grosgrain ribbons are harder to work with and require extra care. Many ribbons will not hold their shape easily with acrylic glazing liquid, so I suggest using fabric glue instead and then using a clothespin or paper clip to apply pressure to the bead on the mandrel until the glue dries.

1 Apply adhesive

Paint a thin layer of fabric glue on the first 1"–2" (3cm–5cm) of the back of the ribbon.

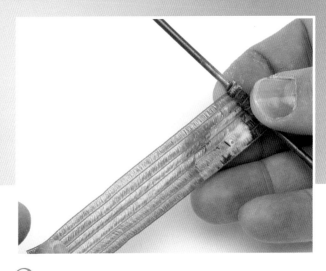

2 Roll bead

Tuck the coated end of the ribbon tightly to the mandrel. Carefully start to roll the ribbon around the mandrel.

Continue to roll the bead until you come to the portion of the ribbon not coated with fabric glue. Brush fabric glue onto the uncoated portion of the ribbon and continue to roll until it is completely wrapped around the mandrel.

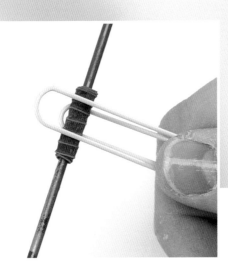

3 Secure ribbon

Hold the ribbon in place using a large paper clip or a clothespin. Let the glue dry completely.

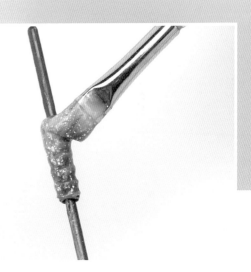

4 Finish bead

Brush a coat of gloss heavy gel on the top of the finished bead and allow it to dry completely. Add another coat of gloss heavy gel onto the bead and let it dry. Paint 2–3 coats of the finishing glaze you have selected onto the rolled bead. Let each coat dry before applying the next coat. If desired, mix glitter into the last coat of finishing glaze before applying it. Remove the dry bead from the mandrel.

materials

11 ¾" (2cm) ribbon
barrel beads

30 5mm bugle beads that
match ribbon beads

54 size 11/0 lavender
seed beads

Beading thread that matches
ribbon beads

Double strand clasp

Size 11 straw needle

Jeweler's cement

TIP

If you gently squeeze the
barrel bead flat, it is easier to
make the needle go straight
through the bead.

Blue Moon Ladder Bracelet

*One of the biggest advantages to working with fabric beads is that you
can sew them together without having to go through the hole in the bead,
which means you can create unique and interesting structures in your
jewelry. I designed this bracelet to show off this feature. The glitter and
luxurious ribbon both add an extra sparkle to the beads for a special
touch of elegance.*

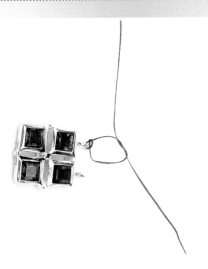

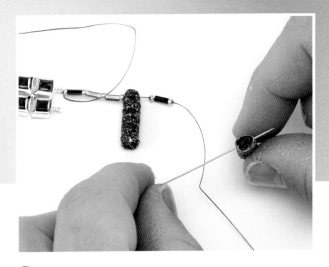

1 Attach clasp

Follow the instructions on pages 36–37 to make 11 ¾" (2cm) ribbon barrel beads. Begin the bracelet by attaching the beading thread to the top connector on the clasp with a surgeon's knot (see *Tying a Surgeon's Knot*, page 26).

2 Begin stringing

Starting and ending with a seed bead, string 4 seed beads and 3 bugle beads, alternating them.

Push the threaded needle through a ribbon barrel bead about 1⁄16" (2mm) from the top edge. String 1 seed bead, 1 bugle bead and 1 seed bead onto the thread. Repeat this beading pattern 10 more times (or less, to make a smaller bracelet). If the bead is stiff use pliers to pull the needle through the bead.

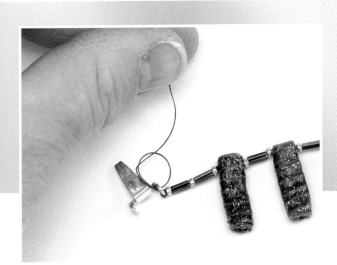

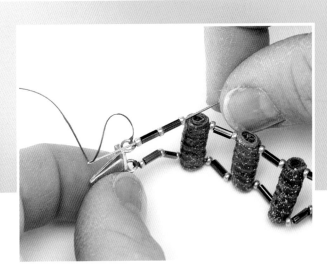

3 Finish first strand

After the last fabric bead is strung, string 1 seed bead, 1 bugle bead, 1 seed bead, 1 bugle bead and 1 seed bead. Attach the second half of the clasp to the end of the bracelet with a surgeon's knot.

4 Attach second strand

Attach a second strand of beading thread to the first half of the clasp with a surgeon's knot. Follow the beading pattern outlined in Steps 2–3 to string the second strand, sewing through the fabric beads about 1⁄16" (2mm) from the bottom edge. Attach the second strand to the second portion of the clasp with a surgeon's knot and hide the beading thread tails (see *Sewing in Tails*, page 28). Secure all knots with jeweler's cement.

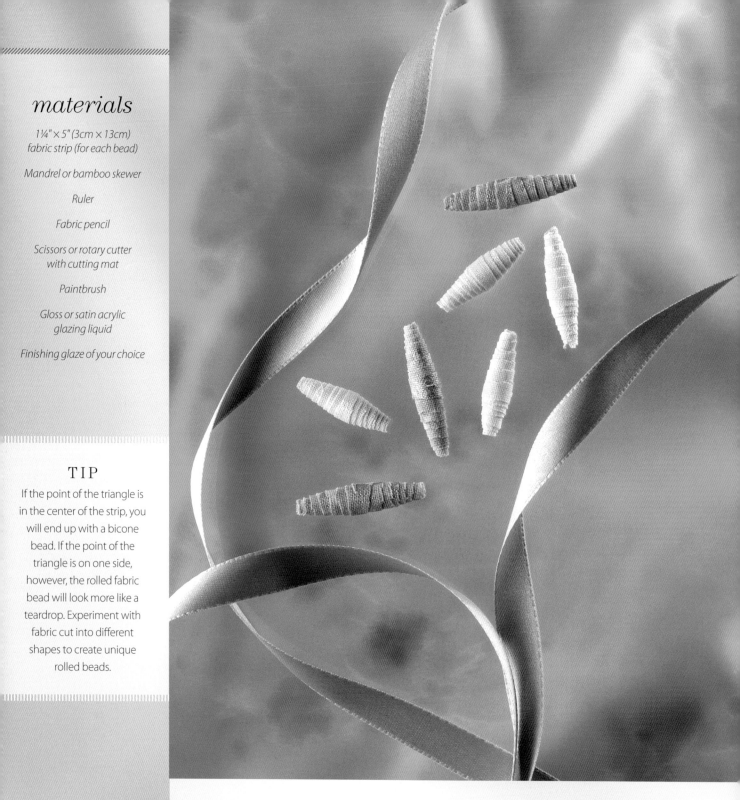

materials

1¼" × 5" (3cm × 13cm)
fabric strip (for each bead)

Mandrel or bamboo skewer

Ruler

Fabric pencil

Scissors or rotary cutter
with cutting mat

Paintbrush

Gloss or satin acrylic
glazing liquid

Finishing glaze of your choice

TIP

If the point of the triangle is
in the center of the strip, you
will end up with a bicone
bead. If the point of the
triangle is on one side,
however, the rolled fabric
bead will look more like a
teardrop. Experiment with
fabric cut into different
shapes to create unique
rolled beads.

Fabric Bicone Beads

*Bicone beads are made using the same technique as other rolled beads, but
the shape of the fabric strip gives them a whole new look. When you cut the
piece of fabric into a triangle, the fabric builds up more in the center of the
bead, creating the bicone shape.*

1 Mark fabric

Fold the fabric strip in half lengthwise, right sides together. Mark the center point at one edge. Open the fabric flat, wrong side up, and put the edge with the mark towards the top. Take a ruler and measure from a bottom corner up to the center mark and draw a line. Repeat with the second corner to form a triangle.

2 Cut fabric

Cut the fabric strip on the drawn lines. Paint a thin layer of acrylic glazing liquid onto the back side of the triangle, starting at the wide end.

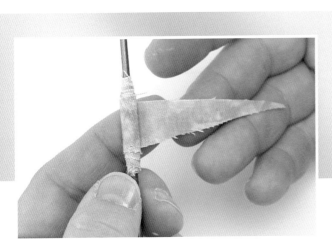

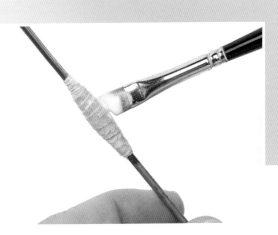

3 Begin bead

Carefully tuck the end of the fabric strip covered with the acrylic glazing liquid tightly around the mandrel. Roll the fabric strip around the mandrel until you come to the fabric without the acrylic glazing liquid. Brush on more of the acrylic glazing liquid and continue to roll until the strip is completely wrapped around the mandrel.

4 Finish bead

Brush another coat of acrylic glazing liquid on the finished bead and allow it to dry completely. Add a second coat of acrylic glazing liquid to the bead and let it dry. Paint 2–3 coats of the finishing glaze you have selected onto the rolled bead. Let each coat dry before applying the next coat. If you would like the bead to have a softer feel, do not put a finishing glaze on top of the acrylic glazing liquid; instead, put a third coat of the acrylic glazing liquid on the finished bead.

materials

8 1¼" (3cm) fabric
bicone beads

6 1" (3cm) fabric bicone beads

1 glass pendant

32 4mm pink AB bicone
crystal beads

17 1mm silver accent beads

30" (76cm) piece
of beading wire

Clasp

2 crimp beads

Crimp pliers
or needle-nose pliers

Wire cutters

Paintbrush

Satin acrylic glazing liquid

TIP

If the pendant you choose
will not fit over the 4mm
crystal beads, string the
pendant on the wire
in place of the center
silver bead.

Lavender Fields Necklace

*The fabrics I used in this necklace already had an iridescent finish, so,
to let the character of the fabric show, I used satin acrylic glazing liquid to
finish the beads instead of a glossy top glaze. This gives the beads a softer
look that helps the necklace have a light and airy feel. The satin finish on
the beads also contrasts nicely with the sparkle from the crystal beads.*

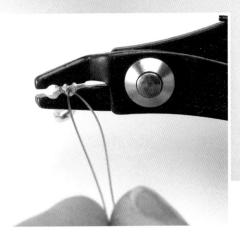

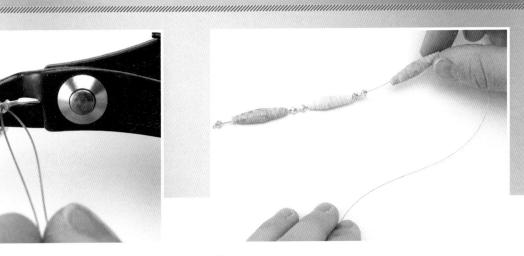

1 Start necklace

Follow the instructions on pages 40–41 to make 8 1¼" (3cm) and 6 1" (3cm) fabric bicone beads. For beads that look like the ones I made, use three coats of satin acrylic glazing liquid as the topcoat. To begin the necklace, slide a crimp bead onto the beading wire about 4" (10cm) from the end. Slide half of the clasp onto the beading wire and loop the wire back through the crimp bead. Use crimp pliers or needle-nose pliers to close the crimp bead in place (see *Using Crimp Beads*, page 22).

2 Begin stringing

Begin stringing the beads onto the beading wire in the following sequence: 4mm crystal, 1mm silver bead, 4mm crystal (abbreviated in this pattern as Crystal/Silver/Crystal combo), 1¼" (3cm) fabric bicone bead, Crystal/Silver/Crystal combo, 1" (3cm) fabric bicone bead. Repeat the beading pattern 3 times.

3 Continue stringing

To create a resting place for the pendant, string beads onto the wire in the following sequence: Crystal/Silver/Crystal combo, 1¼" (3cm) fabric bicone bead, Crystal/Silver/Crystal combo, 1mm silver bead, Crystal/Silver/Crystal combo, 1¼" (3cm) fabric bicone bead and Crystal/Silver/Crystal combo.

To finish the necklace string the remaining beads, reversing the pattern used in Step 2. Finish with a Crystal/Silver/Crystal combo. Slide the pendant to the center of the finished necklace.

4 Complete necklace

Slide the remaining crimp bead onto the beading wire. Slide the second portion of the clasp onto the wire and loop the wire through the crimp bead. Use crimp pliers or needle-nose pliers to close the crimp bead in place. Thread the extra wire at each end through the first few beads for added strength. Trim the excess wire with the wire cutters.

materials

¾" × 5" (2cm × 13cm) fabric strip (for each bead)

2¾" (7cm) piece of 18-gauge dead soft sterling silver wire (for each bead)

Ruler

Extra-fine permanent marker

Wire cutters

Round-nose pliers

Needle-nose pliers

Paintbrush

Gloss acrylic glazing liquid

Self-leveling gel

TIP

If you want to change the size of this bead, change both the width of the fabric strip and the length of the wire. For the wire, add 1" (3cm) for each end loop to the desired length of the fabric bead. For example, if you would like a ½" (1cm) fabric section, add 1" (3cm) for each of the 2 end loops—a 2½" (6cm) piece of wire.

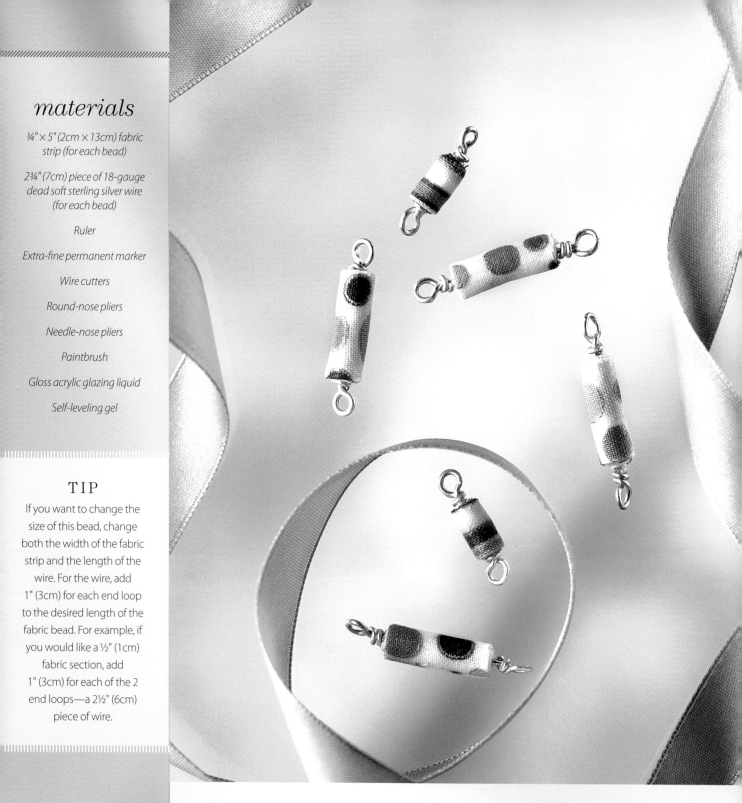

Fabric Barrel Bead on Wire

The wire in these beads acts as a permanent mandrel that the fabric stays wrapped around. These instructions will show you how to make a bead with a simple wire-wrapped end. You can explore other ways to bend the wire at each end to come up with your own style.

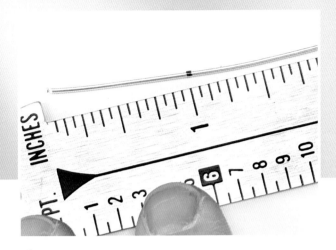

1 Mark wire

Mark the wire with the permanent marker 1" (3cm) from the end. Repeat with the other end of the wire.

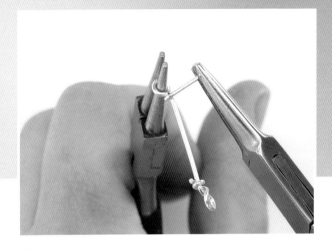

2 Wire wrap ends

Create a wire-wrapped loop at each end of the piece of 18-gauge wire (see *Wire Wrapping*, page 23).

3 Begin rolling bead

Apply a thin layer of acrylic glazing liquid to the back side of the fabric strip for the first 1"–2" (3cm–5cm). Carefully tuck the end of the fabric strip covered with the acrylic glazing liquid tight around the wire between the wire wraps. Roll the fabric strip around the wire until you come to the fabric without the acrylic glazing liquid. Brush on more of the acrylic glazing liquid and continue to roll until the strip is completely wrapped around the mandrel.

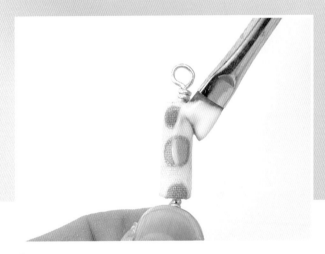

4 Finish bead

Brush another coat of acrylic glazing liquid on the finished bead and allow it to dry completely; since this bead doesn't have a mandrel to dry on, push the wire loop at one end directly into a block of floral foam. Add a second coat of acrylic glazing liquid to the bead and let it dry. Apply 2–3 coats of self-leveling gel to the bead. Let each coat dry before applying the next coat.

Audition the fabric before cutting all your strips of fabric. Just cut one strip and then roll it around the wire before applying the acrylic glaze. Check to see if there is show-through of the print. If you like what you see, cut more strips and proceed with confidence.

NOTES FROM NANCY

materials

*5 ¾" (2cm)
fabric barrel beads
on 18-gauge wire*

*6 ⅜" (1cm)
fabric barrel beads
on 18-gauge wire*

*12 ¼" (6mm)
sterling silver spacer beads*

*12 2¼" (6cm) pieces
of half-hard 22-gauge
sterling silver wire*

Clasp

Wire cutters

Round-nose pliers

Needle-nose pliers

TIP

I recommend wire
wrapping each end of the
18-gauge wire before
cutting the fabric for the
beads in this necklace.
Once the wire is ready,
measure the space
between the loops, then
cut the fabric to the perfect
width to fit the wire.

Candyland Necklace

On this necklace, I varied the size of the beads and the gauge of the wires
to add interest to the design. The choice of fabrics used will set the style of
necklace. I chose a couple of whimsical prints to make a fun, lighthearted
piece. Select elegant fabrics for a more formal necklace.

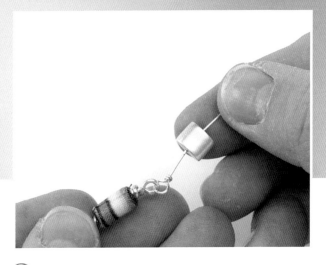

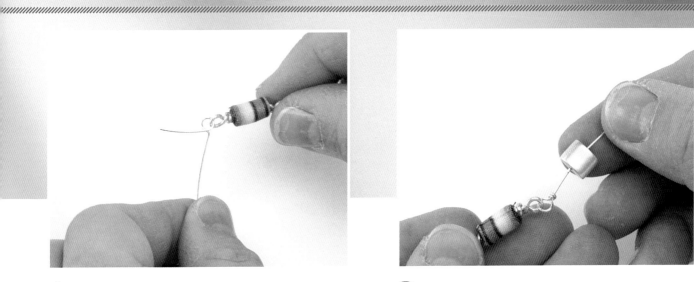

1 Start necklace

Follow the instructions on pages 44–45 to make 5 ¾" (2cm) and 6 ⅜" (1cm) fabric barrel beads on wire. Measure and mark each piece of 22-gauge wire 1" (3cm) from each end. To begin the necklace, wire wrap a piece of 22-gauge wire to a loop on the end of a ⅜" (1cm) bead (see *Wire Wrapping*, page 23).

2 Add bead to wire

Slide a ¼" (6mm) accent bead onto the 22-gauge wire.

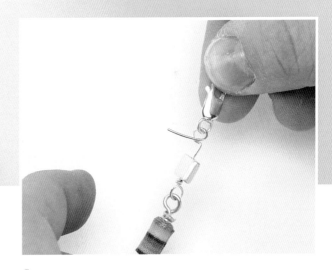

3 Continue necklace

Wire wrap the other end of the 22-gauge wire to a ¾" (2cm) fabric barrel bead on wire. Continue to connect, alternating ⅜" (1cm) and ¾" (2cm) fabric barrel beads on wire with ¼" (6mm) accent beads on 22-gauge wire.

4 Finish necklace

Connect half of the clasp to each end of the necklace with ¼" (6mm) spacer beads on 22-gauge wire.

CHAPTER FOUR

It's a Wrap

The beads in this chapter are wrapped beads, which are constructed over a core. Unlike rolled beads, which get their structure from the fabric being rolled around itself, wrapped beads have a core that gives the bead shape and weight. The projects in this chapter use wood, metal, plastic and fiber as cores.

Wood works well as a bead core because it is not heavy and once the core is wrapped and finished, holes can be drilled into the bead. Being able to choose the placement for bead holes allows design flexibility that you do not get with beads that can be purchased.

Metal is also a good core material for beads. Certain metal pieces can be drilled like wood, depending on the thickness of the metal—test your pieces before you wrap them. I used an assortment of metal washers in the **Hardware Meets Software Necklace** on page 58 that reminded me of the stone donut beads that are available at most bead stores. When wrapping a washer, you can create many different looks just by changing the wrapping materials.

In the **Cute as a Button Bracelet** on page 54, the fabric strips are wrapped around plastic shank buttons. Any buttons or plastic shapes can work for these techniques. Plastic can be slippery to work on, so I recommend lightly sanding the core pieces to help the gels and fibers grip in place.

The last core material is a heavy-weight stabilizer, which is available at most sewing and quilting stores. Choose a stabilizer that is about $1/8"$ (3mm) thick, very flexible and that can easily be cut with scissors. Stabilizer can be sewn through by either hand or machine, opening up different construction options for your jewelry.

Anything you can wrap fabric or threads around that is durable and water resistant will work as a bead core. With the techniques in this chapter, you can create beads in an endless variety of shapes and sizes. Once you have tried your hand at the projects listed here, look for other exciting objects to wrap, such as buttons of various sizes, different wood shapes and found objects that can be sewn or drilled for assembly.

materials

10–12 ⅛" × 2" (3mm × 5cm) fabric strips (for each bead)

¾" (2cm) diameter wood disk

Paintbrush

Drill with ⅛" (3mm) drill bit

Acrylic glazing liquid

Finishing gel of your choice

Awl (optional)

Fabric Wrapped Beads

This bead has a wood disk as its core. I have found wood pieces in many different shapes at craft and woodworking stores that can be wrapped, but a disk is nice and easy for a first wrapping project. Drilling your own holes in the beads allows you to have more control over the final design, as well. Change the width of the fabric strip for a different look.

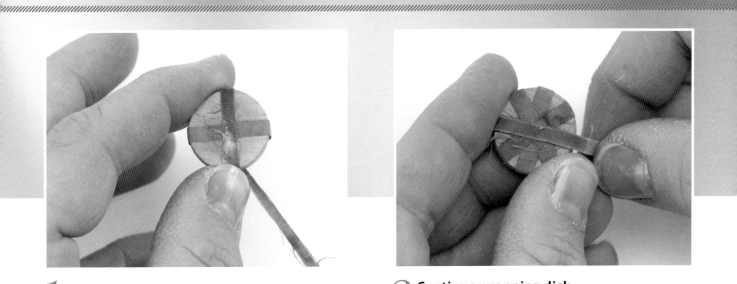

1 Begin wrapping disk

Coat the disk with acrylic glazing liquid. Place the first fabric strip across the middle of the disk with the excess fabric hanging over edges. Paint another coat of acrylic glazing liquid over the strip. Wrap the fabric tails to the back of the disk, overlapping the ends. Paint the acrylic glazing liquid over the tails. Repeat these steps to add a second strip over the first strip, making a cross.

2 Continue wrapping disk

Follow the instructions in Step 1 to add 2 more fabric strips, making an X across the disk.

Another option: use lengths of 2mm silk ribbon instead of cutting fabric strips. If you're like me, you might have beautiful colors of silk ribbon in your stash!

3 Finish disk

Continue to add strips, filling in the gaps on the disk, always crossing the fabric strip over the center of the disk. Once the disk is completely covered, paint another coat of acrylic glazing liquid on both sides of the disk and allow it to dry completely. Add the finishing coat of your choice and let it dry.

4 Drill holes

If you are wrapping a piece that has holes in it, such as a button, use an awl to punch holes in the fabric. If you have wrapped an item without holes, carefully drill a hole into the bead at least ⅛" (3mm) from the outer edge. Add any additional holes that are needed for your jewelry design.

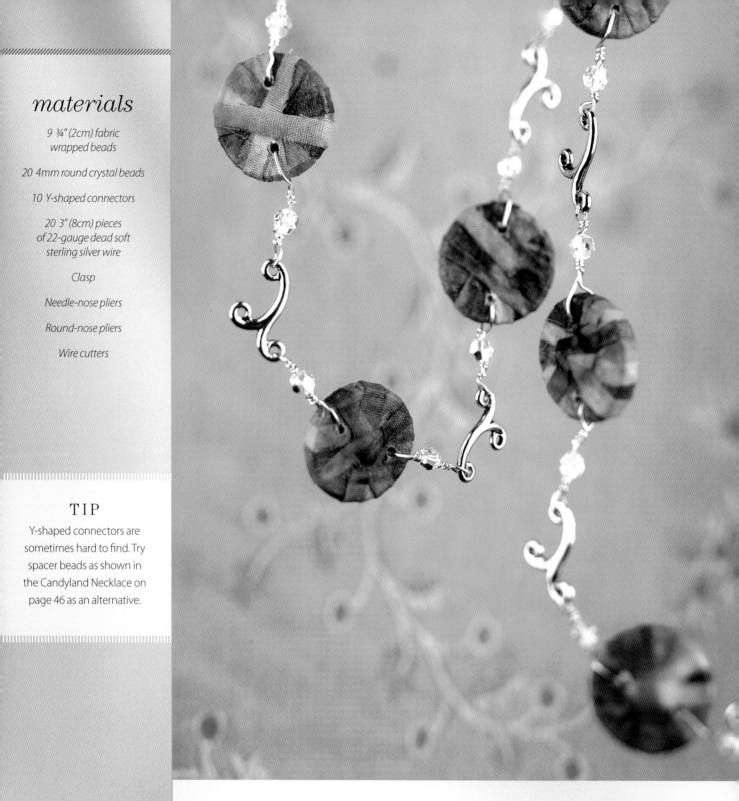

9 ¾" (2cm) fabric wrapped beads

20 4mm round crystal beads

10 Y-shaped connectors

20 3" (8cm) pieces of 22-gauge dead soft sterling silver wire

Clasp

Needle-nose pliers

Round-nose pliers

Wire cutters

TIP

Y-shaped connectors are sometimes hard to find. Try spacer beads as shown in the Candyland Necklace on page 46 as an alternative.

Blue Lagoon Necklace

I combined wire-wrapped crystal spacer beads with fabric wrapped beads for this design. The sparkly crystal accent beads create a nice contrast with the fabric beads. In design, creating contrast within a piece is a great way to add interest to the final project.

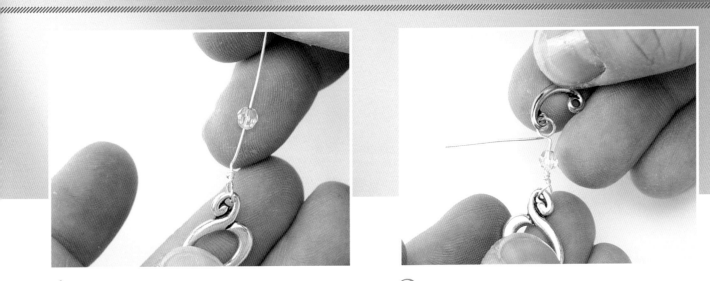

1 Begin necklace

Follow the instructions on pages 50–51 to make 9 ¾" (2cm) fabric wrapped beads, each with 2 holes ⅛" (3mm) from the edge.

Wire wrap a 3" (8cm) piece of silver wire to half of the clasp (see *Wire Wrapping*, page 23). String a 4mm crystal bead onto the silver wire.

2 Continue necklace

Wire wrap the other end of the beaded wire to one side of a Y-shaped connector.

3 Add additional elements

Wire wrap a 3" (8cm) piece of silver wire to the other side of the Y-shaped connector and string a 4mm crystal bead onto the wire. Wire wrap the other end of the wire to a fabric wrapped bead. Continue to add to the necklace, connecting alternating Y-shaped connectors and fabric wrapped beads with wire-wrapped crystals. Keep all of the Y-shaped connectors facing in the same direction.

4 Finish necklace

Wire wrap a 3" (8cm) piece of wire to the last Y-shaped connector. Slide a 4mm bead onto the wire. Wire wrap the free end of the wire to the second half of the clasp.

materials

9 20mm fabric wrapped
shank buttons

200 8/0 seed beads

40" (102cm) piece of brown
beading thread

Beading needle

Scissors

Jeweler's cement

TIP

Try making a bracelet with
each button covered in a
different coordinating fabric
for a scrappy look.

Cute as a Button Bracelet

*The shank buttons I used in this design were very plain when I began. By
covering them with different fabrics, I could match them with anything
I wanted. Being able to custom design your beads is just one of the great
benefits of fabric jewelry!*

1 Begin stringing

Follow the instructions on pages 50–51 to make 9 20mm fabric wrapped shank buttons. Thread a beading needle with the beading thread and add a stop bead to the beading thread (see *Using a Stop Bead*, page 24). String 9 seed beads, 1 button bead and 9 more seed beads on the beading thread.

2 Continue stringing

Run the threaded needle through all of the beads again, excluding the stop bead, to form a loop. Remove the stop bead from the beading thread. Tie the beading thread in an overhand knot snugly against the seed bead loop (see *Tying an Overhand Knot*, page 25). String a second fabric wrapped shank button onto the beading thread. If you are using beads with different designs, alternate them as you see fit.

3 Add additional beads

String 9 seed beads, a third fabric wrapped shank button and 9 more seed beads. Go back through the second button and then through all of the beads strung in this step again. Sew through the first half of the seed beads once more to arrive back at the third button.

4 Complete bracelet

Repeat Steps 2–3 until the bracelet is the desired length. Do not cut the beading thread. String 38 seed beads onto the beading thread. Count from the last button to the 10th bead. Pull the needle back through the 10th bead towards the bracelet to form a loop. String 9 more seed beads onto the beading thread. Sew back through the last button, then follow the thread's path through all of the seed beads after the last button a second time, making a figure eight. Secure the beading thread with an overhand knot. Sew the beading thread ends into the project (see *Sewing in Tails*, page 28). Trim off any extra thread. Add a small amount of jeweler's cement to the knots and allow it to dry completely.

materials

½" (1cm) metal washer

30" (76cm) piece of light
colored rayon floss

10" (25cm) piece of light
colored rayon floss

10" (25cm) piece of dark
colored rayon floss

2 4mm crystal beads

2 6mm crystal beads

Awl

Scissors

Jeweler's cement

TIP

To keep this bead looking
neat, make sure that each
new wrap lies neatly next
to the previous wrap. Once
there is overlap the pattern
is lost and the bead can
look sloppy.

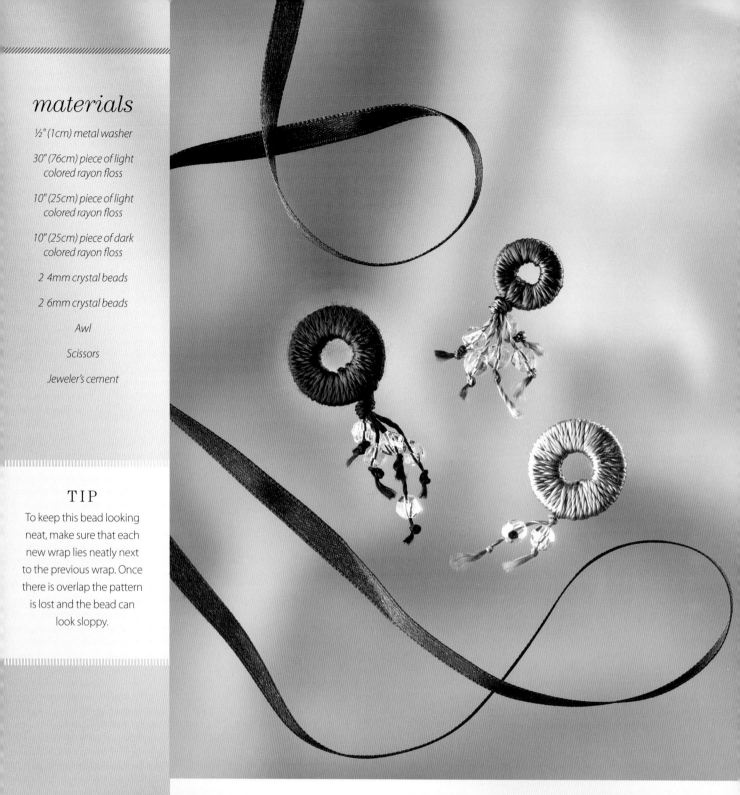

Thread Wrapped Washer

One day when I was fixing something around the house, I noticed that the washers I was using looked just like the popular stone donut beads available today. I decided to wrap the washer with rayon embroidery floss and was happily surprised with the results shown here.

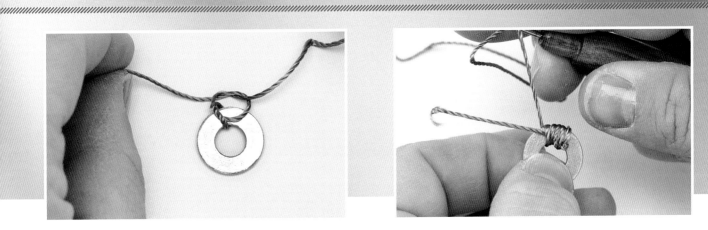

1 Attach floss

Tie the 30" (76cm) piece of floss around the washer with an overhand knot, leaving a 2" (5cm) tail (see *Tying an Overhand Knot*, page 25). To keep the knot tight, apply jeweler's cement to the knot and let it dry completely.

2 Begin wrapping washer

Start to wrap the floss around the washer using an awl to pull the floss through the center of the washer. Wrap the floss around the tail of floss as well for about ½" (1cm). Trim the remaining floss tail off. Hang on securely through the whole process or the threads will come loose and you will have to start over.

3 Finish wrapping

Continue to wrap the floss around the washer, completely covering it. Once the washer is wrapped, pull the floss strand over your finger and behind the washer as shown above . Use the awl to pull the floss tail through the center of the washer. Pull the tail through the loop around your finger and pull tight. Repeat a second time to secure the floss. Use the awl to straighten out the strands of floss.

4 Embellish bead

Tie the 2 10" (25cm) pieces of floss around the washer with an overhand knot at the center of each strand. Thread a crystal bead onto each floss tail and secure the tail with a knot. Add jeweler's cement to each knot to hold them in place. Allow the glue to dry completely and trim the floss tails to your liking.

NOTES FROM **NANCY**

Attention serger owners: 12-weight serger thread could be used instead of rayon floss. This weight of thread is generally used for decorative overlock stitching, yet the weight of thread is ideal for this jewelry–making technique.

materials

1 embellished thread wrapped ½" (1cm) washer

1" (3cm) metal washer

90" (2.25m) piece of light colored rayon floss

90" (2.25m) piece of dark colored rayon floss

30" (76cm) piece of light colored rayon floss

30" (76cm) piece of dark colored rayon floss

Clasp

Awl

Scissors

Jeweler's cement

Hardware Meets Software Necklace

This necklace was made by wrapping two different colors of rayon floss around washers to create beads. I decided to separate the floss tails to braid each half of the chain in a different color, rather then mixing the two colors on both halves of the chain. This subtle effect adds to the overall design. This piece does not need any additional beads to add weight to the piece because the washers also act as weights.

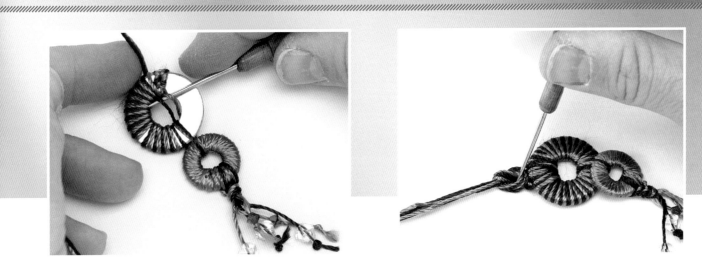

1 Wrap washer

Follow the instructions on pages 56–57 to make a thread wrapped ½" (1cm) washer and embellish it with crystal beads. To wrap the 1" (3cm) washer, tie both 90" (2.25m) pieces of floss around the washer with an overhand knot, leaving a 2" (5cm) tail on each piece of floss (see *Tying an Overhand Knot*, page 25). To keep the knots tight, apply jeweler's cement to the knots and let it dry completely.

Holding the 2 pieces of floss together, wrap them around the washer, using the awl to pull the floss through the center of the washer. Wrap the floss around the floss tails to cover them for about ½" (1cm). Trim the remaining floss tails off. Continue to wrap the floss around the washer, keeping the color order, until the washer is ½ wrapped. On the next wrap, thread the floss through the center of the ½" (1cm) washer. Keep the loop of floss loose enough to let the smaller washer hang below the larger washer.

2 Finish pendant

Continue to wrap the large washer until it is completely covered, then pull the floss strands over your finger and behind the washer. Use the awl to pull the floss tails through the center of the washer. Pull the tails through the loop around your finger and pull tight. Knot the floss strands a second time in the same manner. Use the awl to straighten out the strands of floss wrapped around the washer. You will have 2 long floss tails remaining—do not trim them.

Thread both 30" (76cm) strands of floss through the center of the 1" (3cm) washer. Pull the ends of the strands together so that the floss pieces are folded in half around the washer. Add the long tails left from wrapping the washer to the other 4 tails. Tie all 6 strands together with an overhand knot, snug to the top of the washer, opposite of the ½" (1cm) washer.

3 Braid chain

Separate the light and dark strands of floss. Braid each floss set until the braid measures 9" (23cm) or your desired length. Do not trim the excess floss.

Slide half of the clasp onto each of the braided chains and knot the braids to secure the clasp. Add a small amount of jeweler's cement to each knot and let it dry. Trim the excess floss, leaving a ¼" (6mm) tail.

59

Fabric Sculpted Beads

I wanted to create a bead that looked like draped fabric, but I had to come up with a way to get the fabric to hold its shape. Fusible web is used on the back of these fabric pieces to mold them and help the fabric hold the draped look.

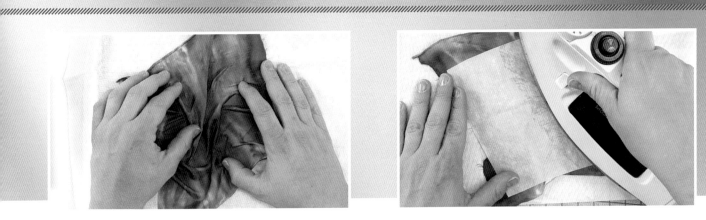

1 Prepare fabric

Cut a 1" (3cm) square from the fabric and fusible web. Following the manufacturer's instructions, press the 1" (3cm) square of fusible web onto the back of the 1" (3cm) square of fabric. Set this piece aside.

Dip the remaining fabric into a cup of water, completely soaking the fabric. Pull the fabric out of the water and ring out any excess water. Place the fabric right side down on the Teflon pressing sheet and scrunch it up to create wrinkles in the fabric.

2 Secure fabric

Place the remaining fusible web on top of the wrinkled fabric, glue side down. Carefully press the fusible web and fabric. Press the iron down without moving it around, then lift and press in another area until you have pressed the entire piece. Once the fusible web is secure, flip the fabric/fusible piece over to the front and press again.

3 Wrap stabilizer

Remove the paper from the back of the fabric/fusible piece and lay it glue side up. Place the 1" (3cm) piece of heavy-weight stabilizer on top of the scrunched fabric with the glue side up. Position the template over a part of the fabric with texture you like, making sure there is at least a ¼" (6mm) of excess fabric around the template. Carefully turn the template and fabric over so the fabric side is up. Press the fabric covering the template in place. Flip the template/fabric piece back over to the template side and trim away the excess fabric, leaving about a ¼" (6mm) of fabric extending past the template. Clip the fabric corners. Pull the excess fabric around the template to the back and press in place.

4 Finish bead

Trim the fabric as needed so none of it can be seen from the front of the bead. Give the piece a good press from the front to make sure everything is secure. Press the 1" (3cm) piece of fabric/fusible to the back of the bead to cover the raw edges.

Don't be alarmed if the silk fabric bleeds when dipped into a cup of water. Often, the fabric is saturated with dye and the immersed fabric will change the color of the water without the fabric losing any visual color.

NOTES FROM **NANCY**

materials

7 1" (3cm) square
fabric sculpted beads

6 ½" (1cm) silver
accent beads

12 4mm blue crystal
bicone beads

2 4" (10cm) pieces of sterling
silver link chain

8 6" (15cm) pieces of beading
thread that match the fabric
sculpted beads

2 sterling silver jump rings

Clasp

Needle-nose pliers

Round-nose pliers

Size 10 straw needle

TIP

Silk gives these beads a
subtle shine, but for even
more sheen use a
gloss glaze.

Silk Sapphires Necklace

*This necklace was made using a small piece of hand dyed silk I had done
as a test swatch many years ago. I was finally able to use it in this necklace,
which only requires a little fabric. These sculpted beads are very light-
weight, but the chain and metal spacers add weight to the piece, both
physically and visually.*

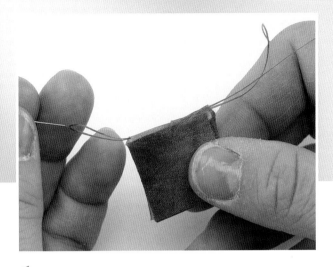

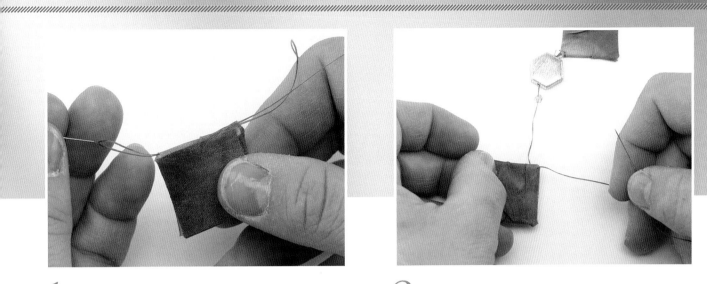

1 Begin sewing

Follow the instructions on pages 60–61 to make 7 1" (3cm) fabric sculpted beads. Thread a needle with beading thread and make a small tailor's knot (see *Tying a Tailor's Knot*, page 24). Sew through a bead, coming out at a corner and burying the knotted thread along the side of the bead.

2 Connect beads

String 1 crystal bead, 1 silver bead and 1 crystal bead onto the beading thread. Sew through the corner of a second sculpted bead. Sew back through the strung beads and the corner of the first bead, then back through the beads again. Take another stitch into the second bead, knot the thread and go back through the beads again. Trim the thread flush with the beads.

3 Add more beads

Repeat Steps 1–2 to attach a third fabric bead to the strand. Create a second strand of 3 fabric sculpted beads. To connect the strands, repeat Steps 1–2 on each side of the seventh bead, attaching it to both strands.

4 Complete necklace

Using the same method used to sew the beads together, sew a 4" (10cm) piece of chain to each side of the necklace. Use jump rings to add half of the clasp to the end of each piece of chain.

materials

5" (13cm) square of fabric

5" (13cm) square of paper-backed fusible web

3" (8cm) square of heavy-weight stabilizer

Mini iron

Teflon pressing sheet

Scissors

Awl

Ruler

Fabric pencil

Craft knife and #11 blade

TIP

Use fabrics with a busy print to hide any seams. Solid colors will show any imperfections in lining up the fabric edges.

3-D Fabric Beads

With my background in industrial design and pop-up paper art, I have always been fascinated with taking something flat and adding dimension to it. I set out to design a 3-D bead that was not fragile and could be worn. By combining heavy-weight stabilizer, fusible web and a little engineering, I was able to build these 3-D beads.

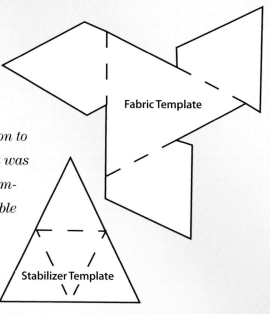

Fabric Template

Stabilizer Template

1 Cut pieces

Trace one fabric template and one stabilizer template onto the paper side of the fusible web. Make sure to trace the dotted lines on the stabilizer template onto the fusible web.

Press the fusible web fabric template to the back side of the fabric. Cut out the fabric on the solid line. Press the fusible web stabilizer template onto the stabilizer. Cut out the stabilizer template on the solid line. Use a ruler and craft knife to score the stabilizer along the dotted lines. Only cut about halfway through the stabilizer when scoring the lines: do not cut through completely.

2 Fuse pieces

Center the heavy-weight stabilizer on top of the fabric, as shown above, with the the scored side of the stabilizer against the fabric and the fusible web side facing up. Iron the pieces together.

When hand sewing the fabric beads your needle, on occasion, might get stuck. Check your kitchen for a rubber jar lid gripper. Use that kitchen gadget with needle and thread as well as the pickle jar!

NOTES FROM **NANCY**

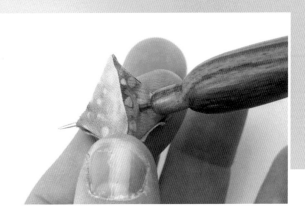

3 Fold bead

Fold up 2 sides of the pyramid along the scored lines in the stabilizer until the edges meet. Wrap the flap of excess fabric that isn't attached to the stabilizer around the joining of the 2 sides; press the fabric in place. Fold up the remaining side to complete the pyramid. Wrap the remaining fabric flaps around the edges and press in place.

4 Finish bead

Trim the excess fabric flush with the edges of the pyramid. Use an awl to poke a hole through the center of one side of the pyramid (this becomes the bottom of the bead), straight up through the opposite pyramid point (this becomes the top of the bead). Slide the awl out of the bead and poke it back through in the opposite direction, starting from the top and going back through the hole on the bottom.

65

materials

5 3-D fabric beads

5 ¼" (6mm) silver disk beads
or bead caps

5 silver dangles

5 3" (8cm) eye pins

7 jump rings

7" (18cm) piece of silver chain

Clasp

Round-nose pliers

Needle-nose pliers

Wire cutters

TIP

You can use a mix of fabric
and metal charms on the
chain to add more interest
to the bracelet.

So Charming Bracelet

*I have always loved charm bracelets, and this is my version of a fabric
charm bracelet. Why not make one with all your favorite fabrics or
fabrics collected from different locations as a memento? There are
so many possibilities with this project. Have fun with it!*

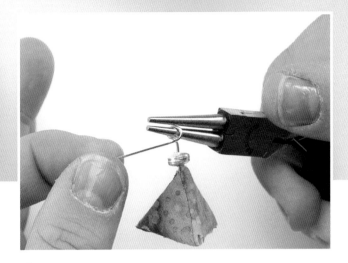

1 Create charm

Follow the instructions on pages 64–65 to make 5 3-D fabric beads. Slide a 3" (8cm) eye pin through the bottom of each bead and up through the top of the bead. Slide a silver disk bead onto the eye pin. Begin to make a wire wrap at the top of the eye pin, but do not complete the wire wrap; stop once the top loop is formed so the charm can later be connected to the bracelet (see *Wire Wrapping*, page 23).

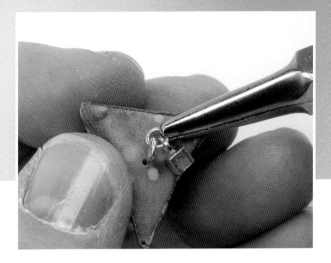

2 Attach dangle

Use a jump ring to add a silver dangle to the loop at the bottom of the eye pin.

3 Attach charms

Lay the chain flat on the table and find the center of the chain. Slide the link at the center of the chain onto the loop at the top of one of the charms. Finish the wire wrap to close the loop at the top of the charm.

4 Complete bracelet

Attach 2 charms to the chain on each side of the center bead, spacing the charms evenly. Use jump rings to add half of the clasp to each end of the bracelet.

CHAPTER FIVE

In Stitches

It seemed fitting to include a chapter on beads that are hand- or machine-sewn in a book on fabric jewelry. The projects in this chapter each reflect the personality of the fabrics chosen for the project; they can be elegant, whimsical or contemporary. Selecting the fabric for your project is an important part of the design process.

If you want an elegant look, such as the **Midnight Sky Necklace** on page 72, think about fine jewelry and its colors, including the many different colors found in gemstones and metals. Look for fabrics that have a metallic finish or consider creating such an effect with paints or other finishes.

For a whimsical piece, like the **Frogs in the Garden Necklace** on page 76, select brighter colors and use a variety of complementary prints together in the same project. Use fun shapes, or try mixing different shapes when designing the project. Select findings that fit the whimsical theme and have fun creating the project.

Contemporary jewelry tends to be simple and bold. Think about these design features when choosing fabrics. Stick with basic colors or subtle prints, and use very plain findings to keep the piece simple. Use only one or two types of beads in the piece.

The beads in this chapter are all created using heavy-weight stabilizer as the core of the bead. This product will not add any weight to the piece, so adding an eyelet or other beads to the construction may be necessary to properly weight the piece.

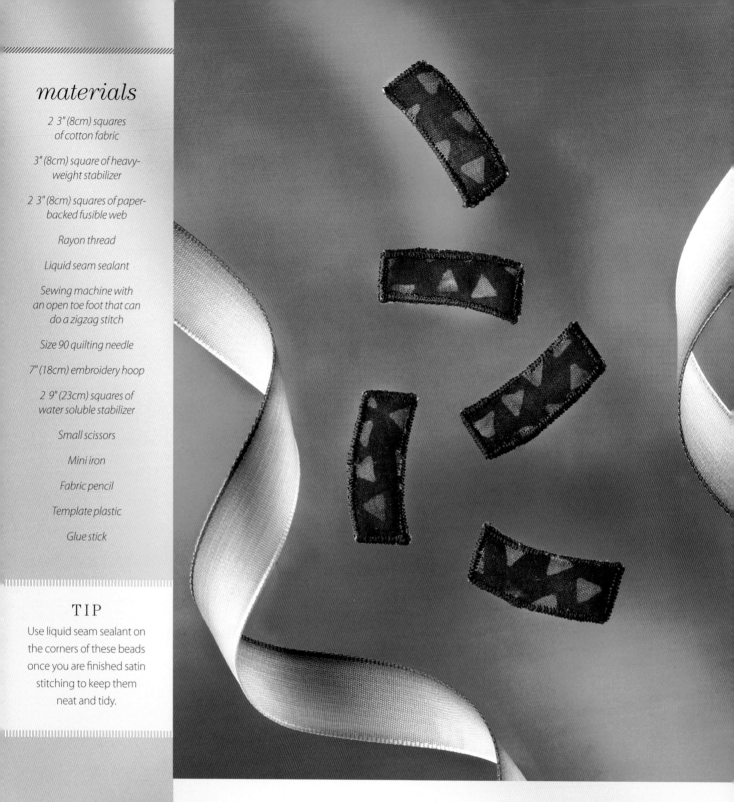

materials

2 3" (8cm) squares
of cotton fabric

3" (8cm) square of heavy-
weight stabilizer

2 3" (8cm) squares of paper-
backed fusible web

Rayon thread

Liquid seam sealant

Sewing machine with
an open toe foot that can
do a zigzag stitch

Size 90 quilting needle

7" (18cm) embroidery hoop

2 9" (23cm) squares of
water soluble stabilizer

Small scissors

Mini iron

Fabric pencil

Template plastic

Glue stick

TIP

Use liquid seam sealant on
the corners of these beads
once you are finished satin
stitching to keep them
neat and tidy.

Fabric Tile Beads

*Fabric tiles can be so fun and fast to make and are only limited by the
shapes you cut from the fabric sandwich. These beads are also soft and
very easy to sew. I did not add a topcoat to these beads, but any of the
coating gels would work well on the tiles. I recommend
that you sew the project together before adding a topcoat
to make assembly easier.*

Tile Template

1 Prepare fabric

Following the manufacturer's instructions, press fusible web onto the back of each fabric square. Press a piece of fabric to each side of the stabilizer square. Create a Tile Template with the template plastic.

2 Trace bead

Trace the Tile Template onto the fabric sandwich with the fabric pencil. Cut out the bead with small scissors.

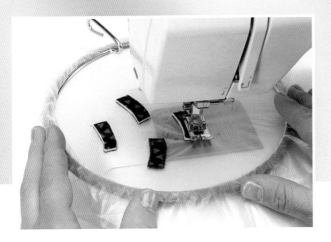

3 Sew bead

Secure both pieces of water soluble stabilizer in the embroidery hoop, making sure the stabilizer is taut. Use a glue stick to add a small amount of glue to one side of the bead; place the bead glue side down on the stabilizer in the hoop.

Set up your sewing machine to do a tight zigzag to make a satin stitch using an open toe foot and a size 90 quilting needle. Practice the satin stitch on a scrap piece of the fabric sandwich until you are happy with the results. The needle should start along the outside edge of the bead and then bite into the bead. This will encase the raw edge of the bead in thread.

Using the embroidery hoop like a steering wheel, satin stitch the edges of the curved bead.

4 Finish bead

Leave the bead on the stabilizer in the embroidery hoop overnight to allow the water soluble stabilizer to dry out. Peel the water soluble stabilizer off the back of each bead. Add seam sealant at the corners or where needed on each bead.

Batik cottons are the fabric that I'd recommend for this great fabric jewelry project. The fabric looks the same on both sides and is tightly woven, eliminating the possibilities of noticeable threads raveling around the edges.

NOTES FROM **NANCY**

materials

14 fabric tile beads

Approximately 425 size 11/0 seed beads that coordinate with the fabric tile beads

26 4mm crystal bicone beads that contrast with the seed beads

1 8mm crystal bicone bead that matches the 4mm crystal beads

Beading thread that matches the seed beads

Beading needle

Scissors

Jeweler's cement

TIP

It is very important to think about what part of the body the piece of jewelry will be worn on when designing the beads. For instance, curved beads like the ones used in this necklace would have a different appearance in a bracelet.

Midnight Sky Necklace

This piece is made using a dark blue batik fabric and crystal beads, with the beads gently curved to follow the wearer's neckline. It reminds me of an ancient Egyptian collar-style necklace, but smaller and easier to wear. Adding additional strands of beads would enhance the resemblance.

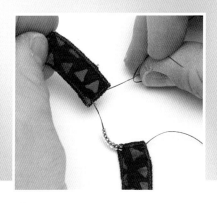

1 Begin first connection

Follow the instructions on pages 70–71 to make 14 fabric tile beads. Cut an 18" (46cm) piece of beading thread. Thread the beading needle and make a tailor's knot at the end of the thread, leaving a 4" (10cm) tail (see *Tying a Tailor's Knot*, page 24). Pull the needle through an upper corner of a fabric tile bead, just inside the satin-stitch edge. Thread 8 size 11/0 seed beads onto the needle, then go through an upper corner of the next fabric tile bead.

2 Complete first connection

Thread 3 seed beads, 1 4mm crystal bead and 3 more seed beads onto the thread. Push the needle back through the upper corner of the first bead, completing a circle of beads joining the fabric tile beads. Run the needle through all the beads again to anchor them in place.

3 Make second connection

The needle should now be on the back side of the first fabric tile bead (the side without the crystal bead) in the upper corner. Push the needle through only the top layer of fabric on the first bead and travel the needle down the short side of the bead and come out at the lower right corner of the first bead. Repeat Steps 1–2 to form a second beaded loop connecting the fabric tile beads.

Tie the bead thread in an overhand knot (see *Tying an Overhand Knot*, page 25). Add a small amount of jeweler's cement to the knot to secure it. Run the needle through the beads again and trim the thread flush with the last bead.

4 Continue necklace

Repeat Steps 1–3 to connect the remaining fabric beads until the necklace is the length you desire. To create each half of the clasp do the following at each end of the necklace: Cut a 12" (30cm) piece of beading thread, thread the beading needle and make a tailor's knot at the end of the thread, leaving a 4" (10cm) tail. Pull the needle through the center of the unconnected edge of the end bead. Thread 6 seed beads onto the thread. Go back through the edge of the fabric tile bead to form a loop. Go through the beads 1½ times, coming out in the middle of the 6 beads. Then:

For the bead end of the clasp: Thread 7 more seed beads onto the thread. Thread the 8mm crystal bead onto the thread. Go back through the 7 seed beads to anchor the crystal bead in place. Go through all the beads again to anchor the clasp in place. Tie an overhand knot at the base of the seed beads.

For the loop end of the clasp (shown at left): Thread 25 more seed beads onto the thread. From the first seed bead, count up 8 beads and go back through the eighth bead to create a loop. Test the loop with the 8mm bead to make sure it is not too small or too large. Adjust the number of seed beads to make a loop that just fits over the 8mm bead. Go through all the beads again to anchor the thread. Tie an overhand knot at the base of the seed beads.

To complete the necklace, sew in all the thread ends (see *Sewing in Tails*, page 28).

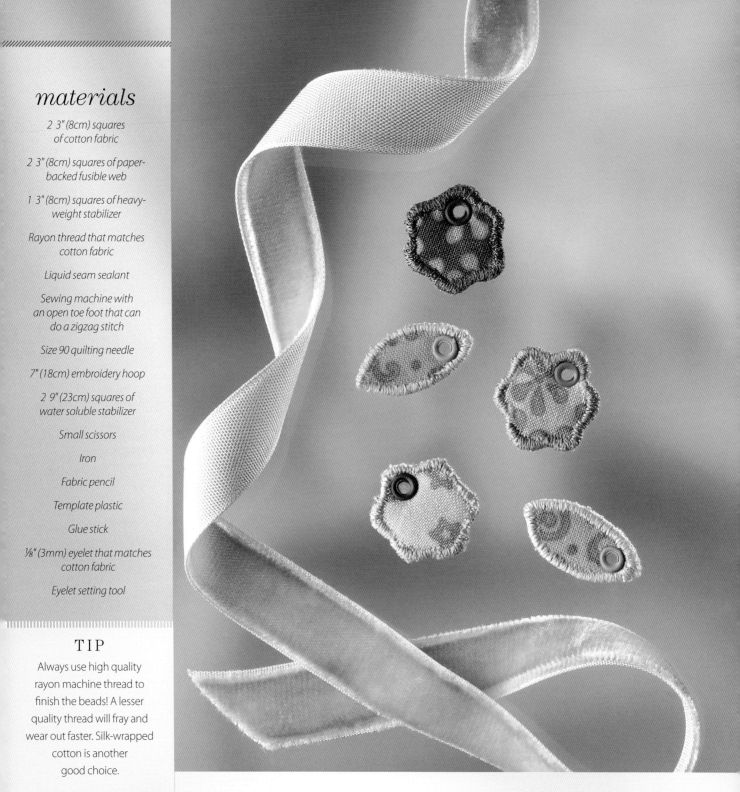

materials

2 3" (8cm) squares
of cotton fabric

2 3" (8cm) squares of paper-
backed fusible web

1 3" (8cm) squares of heavy-
weight stabilizer

Rayon thread that matches
cotton fabric

Liquid seam sealant

Sewing machine with
an open toe foot that can
do a zigzag stitch

Size 90 quilting needle

7" (18cm) embroidery hoop

2 9" (23cm) squares of
water soluble stabilizer

Small scissors

Iron

Fabric pencil

Template plastic

Glue stick

⅛" (3mm) eyelet that matches
cotton fabric

Eyelet setting tool

TIP

Always use high quality
rayon machine thread to
finish the beads! A lesser
quality thread will fray and
wear out faster. Silk-wrapped
cotton is another
good choice.

Fabric Tile Beads with Eyelets

*Instead of sewing fabric tile beads together, try adding
an eyelet to turn the bead into a dangle or charm. Small
eyelets can be found in a rainbow of colors in the scrap-
booking department of most craft stores. These beads can
be elegant or whimsical—it all depends on the fabric,
findings and the shape of the bead used.*

Flower
Template

Leaf Template

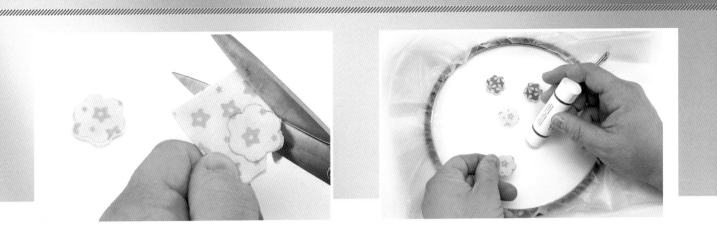

1 Prepare fabric

Following the manufacturer's instructions, press fusible web onto the back of each fabric square. Press a piece of fabric to each side of the stabilizer square. Create a Flower or Leaf Template with the template plastic. Trace the template onto the fabric sandwich with the fabric pencil. Cut out the bead with small scissors.

2 Secure bead

Secure both pieces of water soluble stabilizer in the embroidery hoop, making sure the stabilizer is taut. Use a glue stick to add a small amount of glue to one side of the bead; place the bead glue side down on the stabilizer in the hoop.

3 Sew bead

Set up your sewing machine to do a tight zigzag to make a satin stitch using an open toe foot and a size 90 quilting needle. Practice the satin stitch on a scrap piece of the fabric sandwich until you are happy with the results. The needle should start along the outside edge of the bead and then bite into the bead. This will encase the raw edge of the bead in thread.

Using the embroidery hoop like a steering wheel, satin stitch the edges of the bead. Leave the bead on the stabilizer overnight. The water soluble stabilizer will dry out to make it easier to peel off the back of the bead. Add liquid seam sealant at the edges where needed on each bead.

Using an awl or if your eyelet tool has an ⅛" (3mm) hole punch, punch a hole at the top of the bead just inside the satin-stitched edge. To prevent fraying, do not go through the satin-stitched edge.

4 Finish bead

Following the manufacturer's instructions, set an ⅛" (3mm) eyelet in the hole of the bead.

When satin stitching, it's often recommended to use a light-weight thread in the bobbin and to loosen the top tension by two numbers to assure that the bobbin thread will not be visible on the top of the fabric. Now it's time to change the rules! For this project, use the rayon thread in both the needle and the bobbin, keeping the tension balanced—it's not your grandmother's satin stitch!

NOTES FROM **NANCY**

75

materials

9 flower fabric tile beads with eyelets in a variety of colors

8 leaf fabric tile beads with eyelets

Frog clasp or clasp of your choice

17 10mm sterling silver jump rings

2 6mm sterling silver jump rings

24" (61cm) piece of sterling silver chain

Needle-nose pliers

Round-nose pliers

TIP
Embellish the fabric tiles by sewing seed beads or painting the finished tiles for added sparkle.

Frogs in the Garden Necklace

I love bright, whimsical designs and it shows in my design work. This necklace has a double dose of my design sensibility because I designed the necklace and I designed the fabrics used to make the beads. The inspiration for this piece was the clasp: two sweet frogs clasping hands. I love to collect unique clasps and have them on hand for special pieces just like this.

1 Attach jump rings

Follow the instructions on pages 74–75 to make 9 flower fabric tile beads and 8 leaf fabric tile beads. Open each of the 10mm jump rings (see *Opening and Closing Jump Rings*, page 22). Slide a fabric bead onto each jump ring. Do not close the jump rings.

2 Attach beads to chain

Fold the silver chain in half to find the center link. Attach a flower fabric tile bead to the center link with the jump ring. Then, working from this center point, position the remaining flower beads, alternating them with leaf beads along the chain. Neatly and securely close each jump ring.

3 Attach clasp

Attach half of the clasp to each end of the necklace with a 6mm jump ring.

TIP

I liked the look of size 8/0
seed beads best, but feel
free to experiment with seed
beads in a variety of sizes to
change the look of this bead.

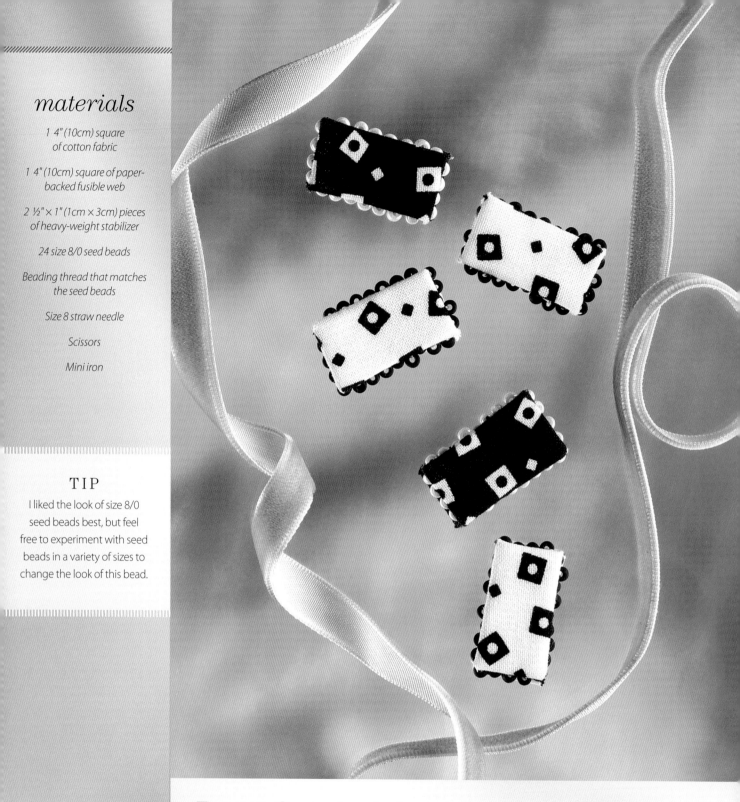

Bead Sandwich

*This bead was inspired by the fabric tile beads. I wanted to add depth to
the bead and experimented with sewing seed beads between two fabric
tile beads. I hid my stitching, but for a different look, you can go all the
way through the fabric tiles and let the stitching show on the right side
of the fabric tile.*

1 Prepare fabric

Press the fusible web to the back side of the fabric following the manufacturer's instructions. Next, press both pieces of stabilizer to the fabric, leaving 1" (3cm) between them. Trim the fabric around each piece of stabilizer, leaving about ½" (1cm) of fabric on each edge. Clip the fabric at each corner.

2 Secure fabric

Fold the excess fabric to the back side of each piece of stabilizer on all four sides. Secure the excess by pressing the fabric to the stabilizer.

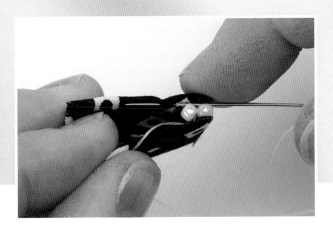

3 Begin sandwich

Cut an 18" (46cm) piece of beading thread and thread the straw needle. Make a tailor's knot at the end of the thread, leaving a 4" (10cm) tail (see *Tying a Tailor's Knot*, page 24). Working on the back side of one of the pieces, push the needle through only the fabric on the back of the piece, starting in the center of the piece and bringing the needle out at a corner.

String a seed bead onto the thread. Go through only the fabric on the backside of the other piece to secure the seed bead between the fabric pieces.

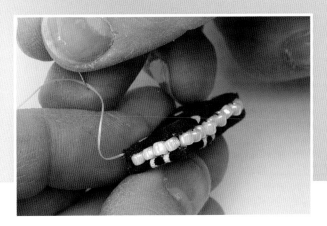

4 Finish bead

Continue to sandwich seed beads between the fabric pieces until you have gone all the way around. Tie off the beading thread between 2 seed beads. Sew back through the bead sandwich to bury the knot and trim the thread.

materials

7 bead sandwiches

16 8mm round
matte onyx beads

Double strand clasp

2 10" (25cm) pieces
of beading wire

4 crimp beads

Crimp pliers
or needle-nose pliers

TIP

For a single strand bracelet,
turn the sandwich beads
lengthwise and only run
one strand of wire through.

Abstract Dominoes Bracelet

Black and white combined together always makes such a dramatic
statement. I used contrasting seed beads in the sandwiches so they
would add to the design and not fade away.

1 Begin bracelet

Follow the instructions on pages 78–79 to make 7 bead sandwiches. Slide a crimp bead onto the beading wire about 4" (10cm) down from one end. Slide a piece of the clasp onto the beading wire and loop the wire through the crimp bead a second time. Use crimp pliers or needle-nose pliers to close the crimp bead in place (see *Using Crimp Beads*, page 22).

2 Begin stringing

String the beads onto the beading wire, starting with a round bead, then alternating bead sandwiches and round beads. End with a round bead.

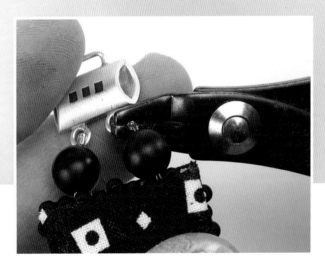

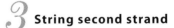

3 String second strand

Attach the end of the top beading wire to the other half of the clasp using a crimp bead and crimp pliers. String the second strand of beading wire through the bottom of the bead sandwiches, stringing a round bead between the bead sandwiches.

4 Finish bracelet

Attach the free end of the bottom strand of beading wire to the other half of the clasp using a crimp bead and crimp pliers.

CHAPTER SIX

Roving Around

Wool is easy to work with and can create stunning results when making jewelry. It is very popular these days, so there is a great variety of wool fabric and roving available in so many different colors and styles. Try different types of wool to decide what you like to work with. There is quite a bit of information out there about wool and what you can do with it. If you like the projects in this book that are made with wool, I recommend checking out other books or magazines, or searching the Internet for more information on working with wool.

The first project in this chapter, the the **Layered Wool Beads** on page 84, is made from layers of wool cloth, while the rest are made from wool roving. Wool roving is made up of wool fibers that have been combed and slightly twisted to prepare it for spinning into yarn. To create wool beads like the the **Single Color Wool Roving Bead** on page 88, the roving is felted; wool fibers felt when agitation causes the fibers to lock together. Agitation can be created through wet felting, which involves rubbing and compacting wool into a form, or through needle felting, when a barbed needle is used to mesh the fibers. Once the wool beads are created, they can be used with other beads, chain, wire and jewelry findings to create beautiful jewelry that can be simple and elegant, sleek and chic or fun and whimsical.

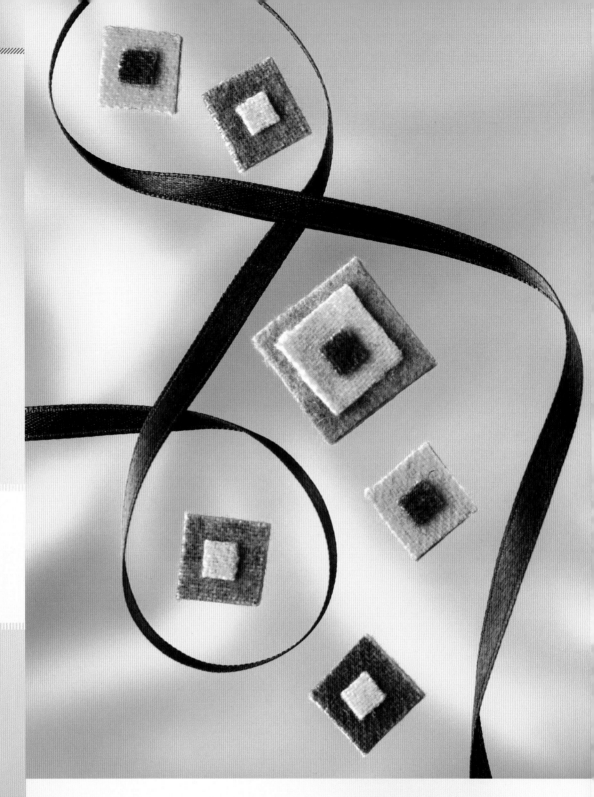

materials

2 3" (8cm) squares
of light colored wool fabric

2 3" (8cm) squares
of dark colored wool fabric

Fabric glue

Paintbrush

Rotary cutter

Acrylic ruler

Cutting mat

Awl

TIP

Use a strong fabric glue;
it will act as a stiffening
agent to keep the beads
from bending or curling.

Layered Wool Bead

*These beads are created by gluing layers of wool fabric together to create
a multicolored, thick wool sandwich that can be cut into different shapes.
The beads are then embellished with small pieces of wool. You can create
other looks with this technique by adding more layers of wool or by
cutting different shapes.*

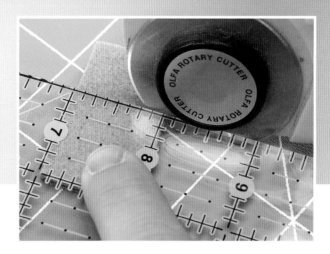

1 Layer fabric

Brush a thin coat of fabric glue on a piece of wool fabric. Place a second piece of wool fabric on top on the glued side and press down. Repeat to glue the third piece of wool on the wool sandwich. You can create a light/dark/light sandwich or a dark/light/dark sandwich. Let the glue dry. If the fabric glue you are using dries quickly, work in small areas and press the wool pieces together as you work.

2 Cut wool

Using the rotary cutter, ruler and cutting mat, cut the wool sandwich into 1" (3cm) squares, or the shape and size you desire.

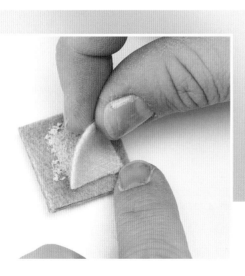

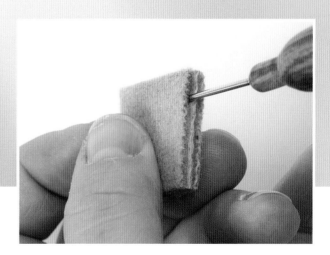

3 Add embellishments

From the remaining piece of wool fabric, cut small pieces for embellishment. Glue the embellishment to the bead. Here, I am adding a ½" (1cm) square in the center of the 1" (3cm) bead.

4 Create holes

To make a hole to string the bead, use an awl and carefully poke it between the back and middle layers of wool, ⅛" (3mm) from the top edge.

materials

5 layered wool beads (see
Step 1 for sizes)

4 ³⁄₁₆" (5mm) silver
spacer beads

22" (56cm) length of sterling
silver chain

Awl

8 silver crimp beads

Crimp pliers (optional)

Needle-nose pliers

Permanent marker

Ruler

Crimp clasp

Jeweler's cement

TIP

If the metal spacer beads
keep sliding while trying to
close the crimp beads, add
a drop of cement into the
spacer bead position on the
chain and let dry. Then
go back and close the
crimp beads.

Violet at Sea Necklace

*This piece was made using hand dyed wool swatches that were just too
precious to waste. I wanted to create a piece where the fabric beads seem
to float around the neck. These fun geometrical beads worked wonderfully
on the sterling silver beading chain. I added the simple metal accent beads
for interest and weight and held them in place using crimp beads.*

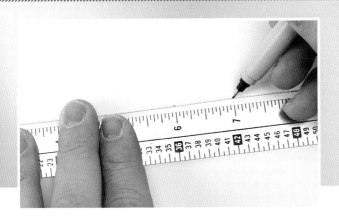

1 Mark chain

Follow the instructions on pages 84–85 to make 5 layered wool beads: 1 1⅛" (3cm) square dark bead with a ½" (1cm) light wool and a ¼" (6mm) dark wool embellishment; 2 ½" (1cm) square light beads each with a ¼" (6mm) dark embellishment; and 2 ½" (1cm) dark beads with a ¼" (6mm) light embellishment.

Fold the 22" (56cm) chain in half and mark the center of the chain with the permanent marker. Mark the chain ½" (1cm) and 1" (3cm) from the center point on each side.

2 Attach first bead

Take the 1⅛" (3cm) square bead and turn it on point. Use the awl to peel back the back piece of wool on the bead at one corner. Slide the chain into the opening and use the jeweler's cement to glue the bead back together around the chain. Let the glue dry completely.

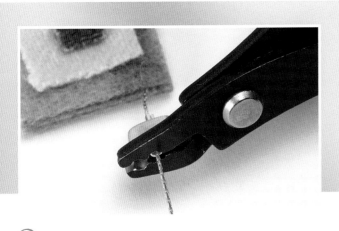

3 Add additional beads

Slide a crimp bead and a ³⁄₁₆" (5mm) spacer bead onto the chain. Center the silver bead over the ½" (1cm) mark on the chain. Push the crimp bead up against the silver bead and crimp it in place (see *Using Crimp Beads*, page 22). Slide a second crimp bead onto the chain and push up against the other side of the silver bead. Close the crimp bead in place. Repeat on the other side of the wool bead.

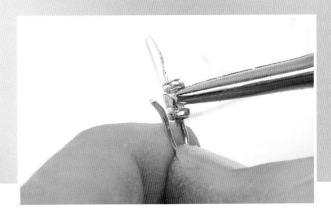

4 Finish necklace

Slide a ½" (1cm) light wool bead onto the chain, aligning the edge closest to the silver bead on the 1" (3cm) mark on the chain. Use the jeweler's cement to glue the fabric bead in place; allow the glue to dry completely. Repeat on the other side of the center bead. Mark the chain again ½" (1cm) and 1" (3cm) away from the light wool beads. Add another silver spacer bead to each side, then ½" (1cm) dark wool beads next to the spacer beads.

Slide half of the crimp clasp onto the end of the silver chain. Using needle-nose pliers, crimp the clasp closed. Repeat with the other half of the clasp on the other end of the chain to complete the necklace.

materials

1 oz. (28g) wool roving

Bowl of warm water

Bar of soap

6" (15cm) square
of bubble wrap

TIP
A round bead is only one
shape you can create using
this technique. Experiment
creating other shapes while
rolling out the beads.

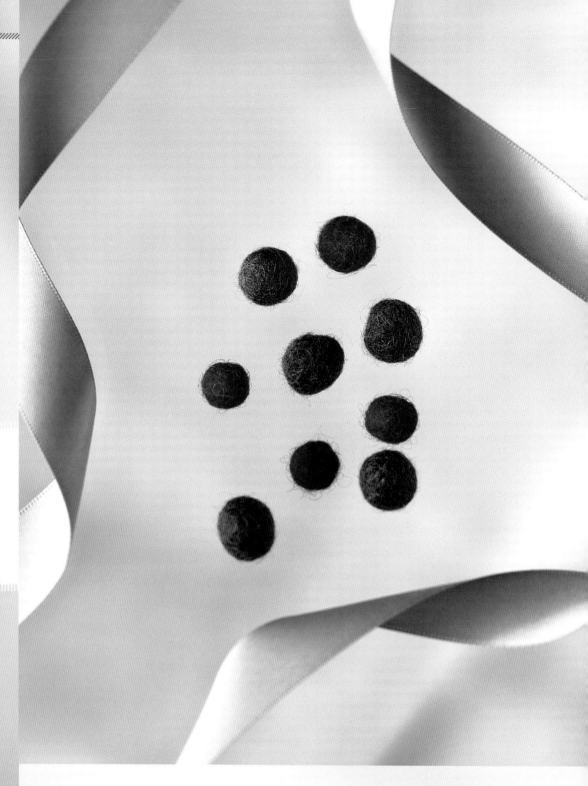

Single Color Wool Roving Bead

*Wool roving beads are simple to make: Just add soap and warm water
to the roving, then rub, rub, rub. I warn you, making these can become
addictive! These beads use one color of roving to keep the bead simple
yet elegant.*

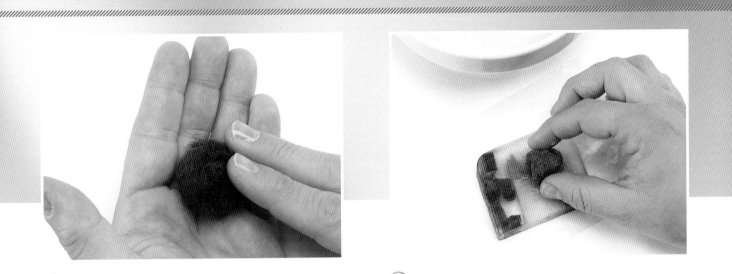

1 Roll roving

Pull off a small amount of wool roving and roll it into a ball in the palm of your hand.

2 Add soap and water

Dip the roving ball into the warm water and gently roll the roving ball on a bar of soap.

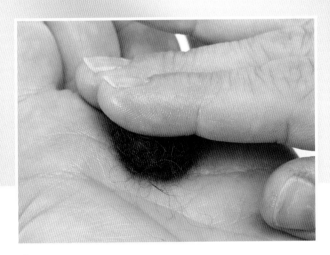

3 Rub bead

Roll the wet ball in between your hands until it is smooth and firm. If the soap makes too many suds, gently dip the bead back in the warm water to rinse.

4 Finish bead

Alternate between rolling the roving in the palm of your hand and on the bubble wrap to help smooth the roving into a bead. Wrap additional dry roving around the bead as you work to make the bead the size you desire. The bead is finished when it is very firm. Rinse any excess soap from the bead and let it dry completely.

NOTES FROM **NANCY**

Check out the DVD and watch Heidi and me create wool roving beads right in front of your eyes. It's a fast technique that brings out child-like creativity!

materials

28 single color wool roving beads, 14 each of 2 colors

35 size 6/0 silver seed beads

Disk pendant with a bail

Clasp

30" (76cm) piece of beading cord

Size 11 straw needle

Awl

Scissors

Jeweler's cement

TIP

Try keeping all your focus beads out in a fabric-lined tray so they are easy to see. Since leaving out my focus beads where I can see them, I have created more pieces of jewelry, just because the beads are sitting there, tempting me.

Raisins and Grapes Necklace

This necklace was one of those rare occasions where I made the beads before I chose the focus bead. I could not believe how well the beads matched each other without any pre-planning. While I love planning designs, a little serendipity can be nice, too.

1 Attach clasp

Follow the instructions on pages 88–89 to make 28 wool roving beads, 14 each of 2 colors. Use an awl to make a hole through each bead. Tie the beading cord to half of the clasp using an overhand knot, leaving a 2" (5cm) tail (see *Tying an Overhand Knot*, page 25). Add a bit of jeweler's cement to the knot and let it dry completely.

2 Begin stringing

Begin stringing the beads, alternating wool beads with seed beads, and alternating the colors of the wool beads.

3 Add pendant

After stringing 12 wool beads, string 3 seed beads in a row. Slide the disk pendant over the 3 seed beads.

4 Finish necklace

Repeat Step 2 to string the second half of the necklace. Tie the other half of the clasp to the end of the beading cord and secure the knot with jeweler's cement. Thread each bead cord tail on the needle and sew the tails into the beads. Trim off the cord tails.

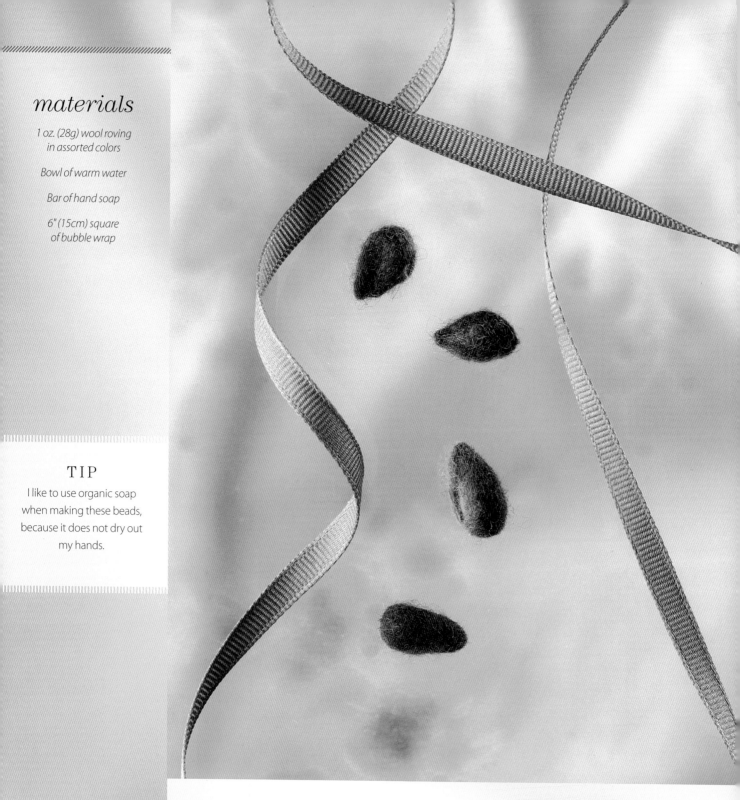

materials

1 oz. (28g) wool roving
in assorted colors

Bowl of warm water

Bar of hand soap

6" (15cm) square
of bubble wrap

TIP

I like to use organic soap
when making these beads,
because it does not dry out
my hands.

Multicolor Wool Roving Bead

When working with roving, it is very easy to blend colors to make a piece that looks like swirls of paint. This effect is achieved by blending different colors of roving before making the beads. Just make sure to blend enough roving before rolling the beads so all the beads match!

1   Mix roving

Lay small amounts of each color of roving on the table with the fibers laying in the same direction. Grasp one end of the pile in each hand and gently pull the roving apart so that you now have two stacks of roving. Lay one over the other. Repeat layering and pulling until the roving is mixed as you desire.

2   Add soap and water

Pull off a small amount of the mixed wool roving and roll into a ball in the palm of your hand. Dip the roving ball into the warm water and gently roll the roving ball on a bar of soap.

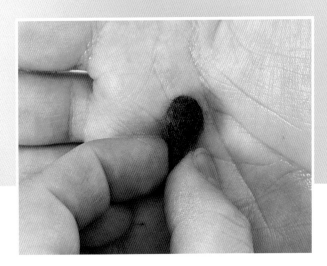

3   Felt roving

Roll the wet ball in between your hands until it is smooth and firm. If the soap makes too many suds, gently dip the bead back in the warm water to rinse. Alternate between rolling the roving in the palm of your hand and on the bubble wrap to help smooth the roving into a bead.

4   Shape bead

Once the ball is fairly firm, shape it into a teardrop, then continue felting it. You will know the bead is finished when it is very firm. Rinse any excess soap from the bead and let dry.

materials

7 multicolor teardrop
wool roving beads

190 gold triangle seed beads

Clasp

30" (76cm) piece
of beading wire

Two crimp beads

Crimp pliers
or needle-nose pliers

Awl

Tapestry needle

TIP
One trick to making
consistently sized beads is
to roll roving into a log, then
cut it into equal segments
and roll the beads into the
desired shape.

Phoenix Rising Necklace

*This piece was a last-minute addition to the book. Because I created it
out of what I had with me on a trip (yes I travel with bead supplies sometimes!), I felt the name fit not only the colors, but how the project came
about. Five different colors of roving (donated by my wonderful editor,
Jenni) were blended together to create these beautiful teardrop beads.*

1 Prepare beads

Follow the instructions on pages 92–93 to make 7 multi-color wool roving beads: 1 ⅞" (2cm) teardrop, 2 ¾" (2cm) teardrops, 2 ½" (1cm) teardrops and 2 ⅜" (1cm) teardrops. Use an awl and make a hole at the top of each bead.

2 Start stringing

Thread the beading wire onto the tapestry needle. Use the needle to string the ⅞" (2cm) wool teardrop bead onto the wire.

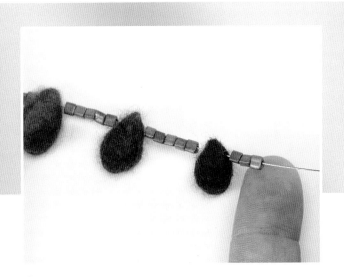

3 Continue stringing

Remove the needle from the bead wire and thread 5 seed beads onto the wire on each side of the ⅞" (2cm) bead. Rethread the needle with the beading wire and string a ¾" (2cm) bead on each side of the necklace. Add 5 more seed beads to each side, and then add the ½" (1cm) wool teardrop beads. String 5 more seed beads on each side of the necklace.

4 Finish necklace

String a ⅜" (1cm) wool tear drop bead on each side of the necklace. Next, string 63 seed beads on each side of the necklace. Attach half of the clasp to each end of the necklace with crimp beads (see *Using Crimp Beads*, page 22).

materials

1 oz. (28g) wool roving
in assorted colors

Bowl of warm water

Bar of hand soap

6" (15cm) square
of bubble wrap

Felting needle

TIP

To give your needle felted
beads a smooth, polished
look, you can re-wet and
reroll them to felt the surface fibers tightly together.

Needle Felted Beads

*If you want to embellish wool beads, needle felting is the way to go. A felting
needle has barbs along its length, which push small amounts of wool roving
into the ball. The barbs on the roving fibers tangle with the barbs on the bead
fibers, holding everything in place. You can make your own beads as the
base or purchase some wool beads to needle felt.*

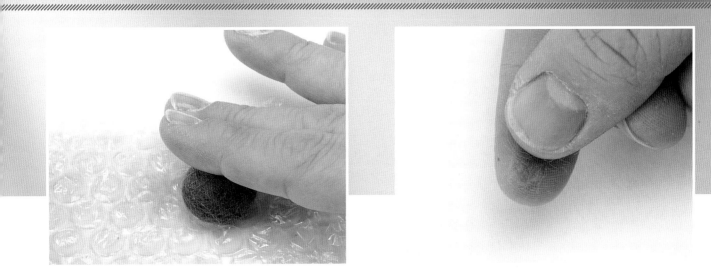

1 Create base

Follow the instructions on pages 88–89 to make wool roving beads in your choice of sizes and colors.

2 Prepare embellishments

Pull off very small amounts of roving to create embellishments. For dots, roll the roving into small balls. For stripes, roll the roving into a snake.

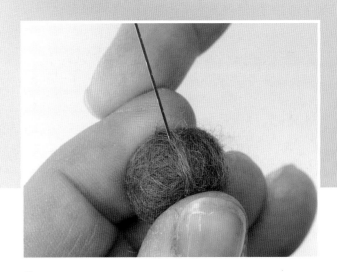

3 Add dots

To add dots to a bead, place the rolled roving on the wool ball. Using the felting needle, poke up and down on the dot until it is secure on the wool bead. Watch your fingers because felting needles are very sharp! Repeat to attach as many dots as desired.

4 Add stripes

To add stripes, lay the roving on top of the bead and wrap it around the bead to make a stripe, overlapping the ends of the roving. Use the felting needle to push the stripe into the bead, poking the needle repeatedly into each part of the stripe.

materials

3 needle felted beads

2 ¼" (6mm) sterling silver spacer beads

3 1/8" (3mm) sterling silver dangle beads

1 ½" (1cm) sterling silver bead cap

4½" (11cm) piece of 18 gauge sterling silver dead soft wire

3 4mm jump rings

1 8mm jump ring

24" (61cm) sterling silver chain with clasp

Awl

Needle-nose pliers

Round-nose pliers

TIP
You can find wool beads from manufacturers that are ready to be embellished with needle felting.

The Jester Necklace

This necklace reminds me of what a court jester would wear on her night out on the town, using jewel tones instead of bright colors to make the piece look sophisticated. The colors used in a piece of jewelry set the mood and overall look of the piece, so choose carefully. Look at your own clothing choices or fashion magazines for color inspiration.

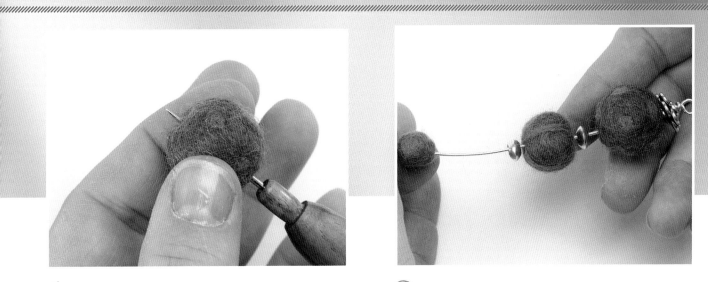

1 Prepare beads

Follow the instructions on pages 88–89 to make 1 ¼" (6mm), 1 ½" (1cm) and 1 1" (3cm) wool roving beads. Follow the instructions on pages 96–97 to embellish the ½" (1cm) and 1" (3cm) beads. Use an awl to poke a hole through the center of each bead.

2 Begin pendant

Create a wire-wrapped loop at the end of the 4½" (11cm) piece of wire (see *Wire Wrapping*, page 23). Slide the bead cap onto the wire followed by the 1" (3cm) wool bead, then a ¼" (6mm) spacer bead, then the ½" (1cm) wool bead, a second ¼" (6mm) spacer bead and the ¼" (6mm) wool bead.

3 Finish pendant

Create a wire-wrapped loop at the open end of the silver wire. Open the 8mm jump ring and add it to the top loop on the pendant (see *Opening and Closing Jump Rings*, page 22).

4 Finish necklace

Using 4mm jump rings, add each ⅛" (3mm) dangle bead to the bottom loop on the pendant. Slide the completed pendant onto the chain.

CHAPTER SEVEN

Braided and Knotted

This final chapter of projects explores not only beads made from cords and yarns, like the **Square Knot Bead** on page 114, but chains made from fibers, as well, such as the **Double Braided Chain** on page 106. With so many wonderful yarns, cords and trims available today at craft, needlepoint and knitting stores it is easy to find different fibers to create stunning pieces of jewelry. Cords, yarns and trims can become just as addictive to buy and collect as fabric and beads. Believe me—I have the stash to prove it!

The most important things to consider when picking fibers to work with is how they feel on your skin and how durable they are. I recommend tying a couple of pieces of the fibers around your wrist and wearing them for a day. If they are uncomfortable, you will know right away and don't have to continue with the experiment. But, if the fibers feel good against your skin, continue to wear them throughout the day to see how well they hold up to being worn. Some trims may start to fray, and others will look dirty just from the oils from your skin or from attracting dirt through the day. This may seem like an unnecessary step, but there is nothing more frustrating than working on a piece of jewelry that does not last or looks bedraggled after the first time it is worn. Testing fibers before using them in a project will save you time and frustration.

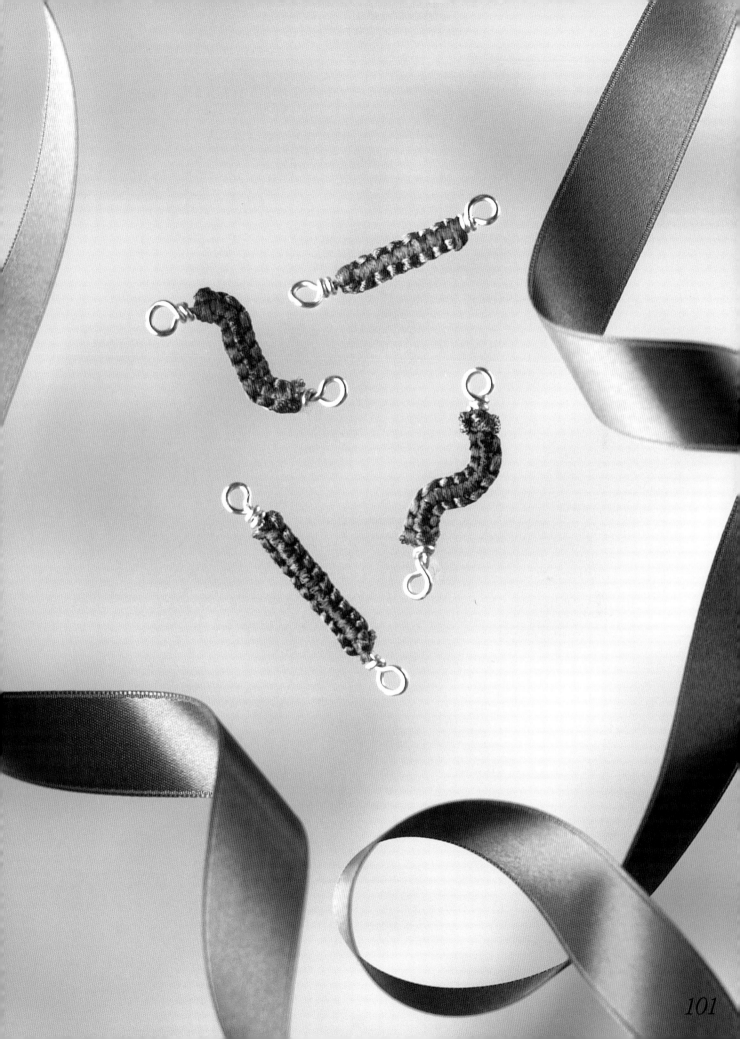

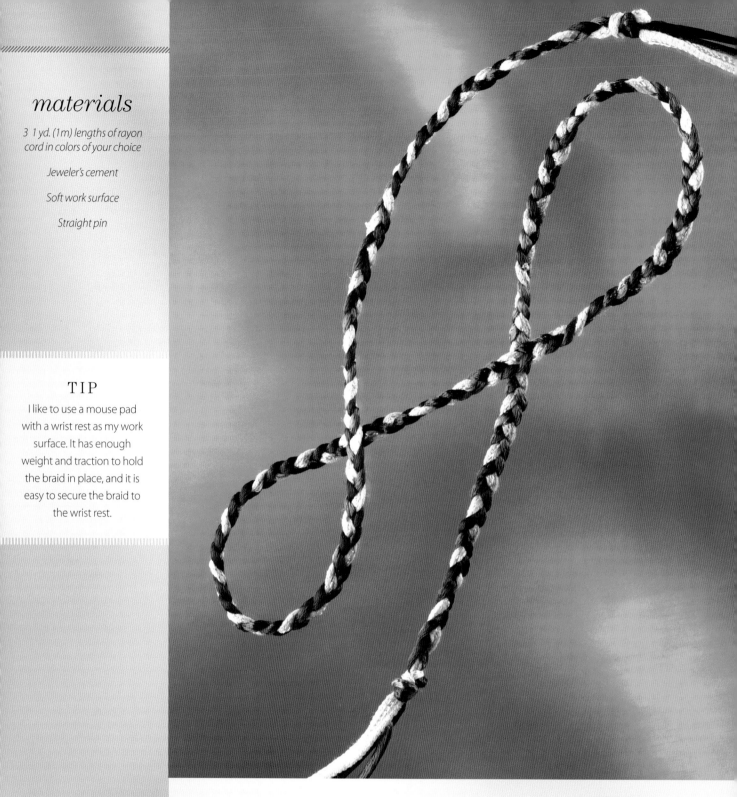

materials

3 1 yd. (1m) lengths of rayon cord in colors of your choice

Jeweler's cement

Soft work surface

Straight pin

TIP

I like to use a mouse pad with a wrist rest as my work surface. It has enough weight and traction to hold the braid in place, and it is easy to secure the braid to the wrist rest.

Single Braided Chain

Most of us learned how to do a single braid as a child. I experimented with different ways to make a cord chain for this book and I kept coming back to the simple braid. There is something elegant about a braid and it works so well as a chain; you can also match your braid to the focus beads in the project for a pulled-together look.

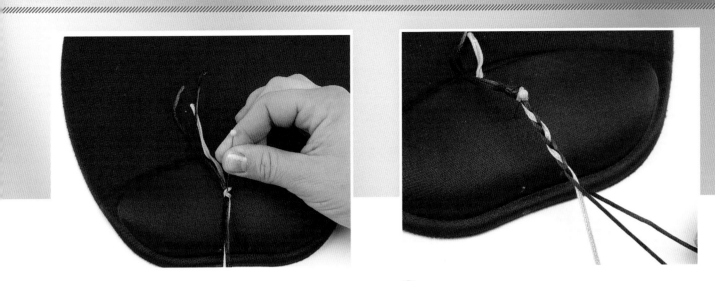

1 Secure cord

Tie the 3 strands of rayon cord together with an overhand knot (see *Tying an Overhand Knot*, page 25). Add a drop of jeweler's cement to the knot and let it dry. Secure the knotted strands to your work surface with a straight pin.

2 Begin braiding

Separate the 3 strands of cord. To start the braid, cross the left strand over the center strand—the strand that started on the left is now the center strand, and the strand that started as the center strand is now the left strand.

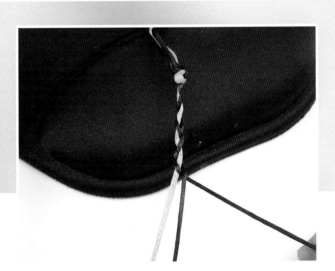

3 Continue braiding

Next, cross the right strand over the center strand. Continue to braid by alternately crossing the left strand over the center strand, then the right strand over the center strand.

4 Finish braiding

Continue to braid the strands until the braid is 22" (56cm) long. Tie the 3 strands together in an overhand knot at the end of the braid. Add a drop of jeweler's cement to the knot and let it dry.

materials

22" (56cm) length
of single braided chain

1 1¼" (3cm) square
glass bead

1 ¾" (2cm) round glass bead

2 sterling silver terminators

2 5" (13cm) pieces
of beading wire

4 crimp beads

Lobster claw clasp

4mm spring ring

Crimp pliers
or needle-nose pliers

Industrial strength craft
adhesive

TIP

When using a fiber cord,
make sure the pendant used
has enough weight to pull
the necklace down.

Sedona Mountains Necklace

*I bought several glass beads that reminded me of batik fabric because of
the way the colors swirled through the glass. For this piece, I found a dark
cord and a light cord that matched the beads and used them for the chain.
Though this is one of the simplest pieces in the book, it is my favorite and
I find myself wearing it often.*

1 Attach beading wire

Follow the instructions on pages 102–103 to make a 22" (56cm) single braided chain. Slide a 5" (13cm) piece of beading wire through the knot at the end of the braid. Make a loop with the wire and secure it with a crimp bead (see *Using Crimp Beads*, page 22).

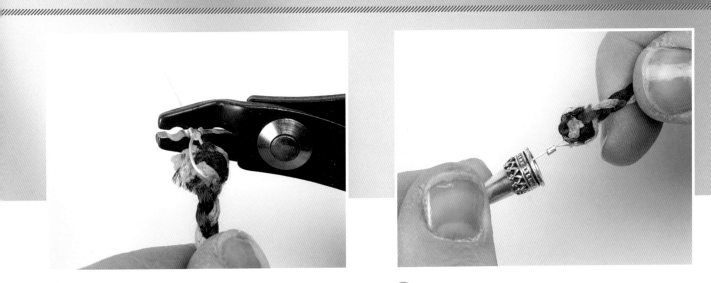

2 Attach terminator

Slide the beading wire and the knot into a sterling silver terminator. Glue the knot into the terminator with the industrial strength craft adhesive. Repeat on the other end of the necklace.

3 Attach clasp

Slide a crimp bead and the lobster claw clasp onto the beading wire. Close the crimp bead. Repeat on the other side of the braided chain with a crimp bead and spring ring.

4 Attach beads

Attach both beads to the center of the single braided chain with a half-hitch knot (see *Tying a Half-Hitch Knot*, page 27).

materials

6 2 yd. (2m) strands of floss

2 44" (112cm) strands of rayon cord

Jeweler's cement

Soft work surface

Straight pin

TIP

When working on an extra long braid, tie one end to a doorknob and pull gently as you braid to keep the strands from tangling.

Double Braided Chain

This chain is a variation on the single braid. I first braided thin thread to make one of the cords for the final braid. You can build braided cord on braided cord as many times as you wish to make a thicker chain.

1 Create single braid

Tie all 6 strands of floss together with an overhand knot (see *Tying an Overhand Knot*, page 25). Secure the knot with a drop of jeweler's cement. Separate the 6 strands into 3 pairs of strands. Follow the instructions on pages 102–103 to make a 44" (112cm) single braided chain.

2 Begin double braid

Tie the floss single braided chain and the 2 strands of rayon cord together with an overhand knot 4" (10cm) from the end of the strands. Secure the knot with a drop of jeweler's cement. Allow the glue to dry completely.

3 Continue double braid

Follow the instructions on pages 102–103 to braid the 2 strands of cord and 1 single braid together.

4 Finish braid

Braid until approximately 4" (10cm) of cord remain. Tie the strands together in an overhand knot at the end of the braid. Add a drop of jeweler's cement to the knot and let it dry.

materials

24" (61cm) double braided
chain

Funnel bead

12 6mm crystal beads

Collapsible eye needle

Awl

Scissors

Jeweler's cement

TIP

If you wanted to create a
piece that is made entirely
from fibers and fabric, you
could make your funnel
bead using heavy-weight
stabilizer covered in fabric.

Star Cluster Necklace

*I used a glass bead cap as my funnel bead for this project, but the funnel
bead can be anything you like. I also attached crystals to the ends of
the cords for added interest and weight. You could use charms or an
assortment of different beads to add weight to your piece.*

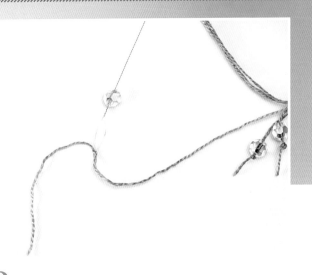

1 Trim cords

Follow the instructions on pages 106–107 to make a 24" (61cm) double braided chain with a 4" (10cm) tail at each end of the braid. Trim cord tails to ½" (1cm) on each of the braids. Do not trim the single braided chain tails.

2 Begin attaching beads

Using a collapsible eye needle, string a 6mm crystal bead onto a floss tail.

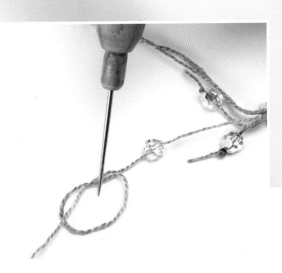

3 Secure beads

Tie each beaded strand with an overhand knot, guiding the knots to sit at different lengths with the awl (see *Tying an Overhand Knot*, page 25). Secure each knot with a drop of jeweler's cement; allow the glue to dry completely.

4 Finish necklace

Fold the double braided chain in half and slide the looped end of the chain into the funnel bead. Pull the funnel bead down onto the crystal cluster.

materials

4" (10cm) piece
of 18 gauge silver wire

30" (76cm) length
of ribbon or cord

Ruler

Permanent marker

Needle-nose pliers

Tapestry needle

TIP

For variety, bend your wire
into different shapes before
you begin knotting.

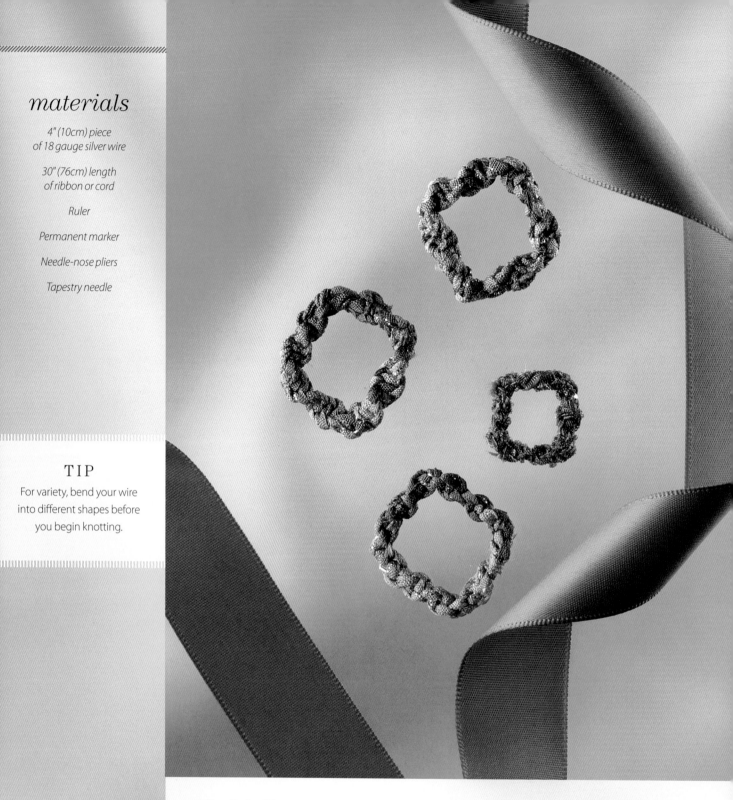

Half-Square Knot Bead

As a little girl in the 1970s, I was exposed to large amounts of macramé, mostly by my dad. Even though macramé went out of style, I never forgot sitting there with my dad, practicing square knots. I always loved how the half-square knots would twist as you made them. This memory inspired me to make these beads by working half-square knots around a piece of wire bent into a square.

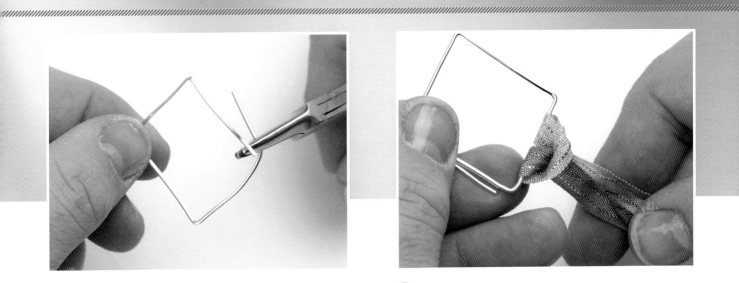

1 Bend frame

Mark the 4" (10cm) piece of wire in ¾" (2cm) increments across the length of the wire. Bend the wire into a square using the marks as the corner points. There will be a small overlap of wire.

2 Attach ribbon

Fold the piece of ribbon in half. Tie the ribbon to the wire square using a half-hitch knot on the side before the over-lapped wire (see *Tying a Half-Hitch Knot*, page 27).

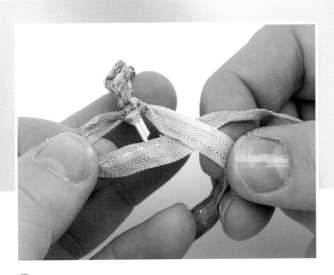

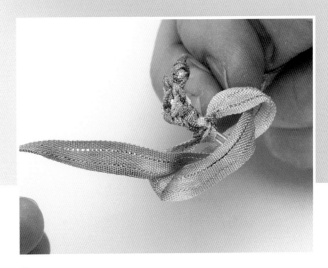

3 Begin knotting

Separate the strands of ribbon with the wire in the center. Take the ribbon on the left side and pull it to the right over the wire and under the left ribbon.

4 Finish bead

Pull the right ribbon under the left ribbon and the wire, then up through the loop of ribbon on the left side of the wire. Pull the knot snug around the wire.

Continue to tie knots around the wire square. The knots will start to twist around the wire square—this is what the knot does naturally, so let it twist. Once the wire square is completely covered, thread each ribbon tail onto the tapestry needle and sew the tail into the bead (see *Sewing in Tails*, page 28).

materials

6 half-square knot beads

20 size 11/0 seed beads
that match the half-square
knot beads

10 6mm sterling silver
disk beads

Clasp

Beading cord

Straw needle

1" (3cm) cylinder or tube

TIP
Keep your tension even
as you knot for a
consistent look.

Midsummer Night's Dream Bracelet

I found the gorgeous variegated ribbon used in this project at a vintage trim and ribbon company. I loved the ethereal look and feel of the ribbon and knew I wanted to make a delicate piece with it. I also used a sage rayon ribbon to complement the variegated ribbon in this piece. For bracelets, adding weight to the piece is not as important as it is with other types of jewelry, but the shape of the bead is. I gently bent each bead to have a slight curve to fit against a wrist so the piece is more comfortable to wear.

1 Prepare beads

Follow the instructions on pages 110–111 to make 6 half-square knot beads: 3 ¾" (2cm) variegated square beads and 3 ½" (1cm) single color square beads. Gently bend each bead on a 1" (3cm) cylinder or tube to give each bead a slight curve. This will make the bracelet lay correctly on your wrist.

2 Begin connecting beads

Thread the beading cord onto the straw needle. Pull the needle through the ¾" (2cm) square bead, coming out at the upper right corner approximately ⅛" (3mm) from the top edge. Slide 1 11/0 seed bead, 1 6mm silver disk bead and 1 11/0 seed bead onto the beading cord. Sew through the upper left corner of a ½" (1cm) square bead.

3 Complete first connection

Travel down the side of the ½" (1cm) square bead to come out at the lower left corner. Slide 1 size 11/0 seed bead, 1 6mm silver disk bead and 1 size 11/0 seed bead onto the beading cord. Sew through the lower right corner of the ¾" (2cm) square bead to connect the 2 square beads. Tie a knot and sew in the tail of the thread (see *Sewing in Tails*, page 28).

4 Finish bracelet.

Repeat Steps 2–3 to connect all the square beads, alternating the ¾" (2cm) and ½" (1cm) beads. Use the same method to sew half of the clasp to each end of the bracelet.

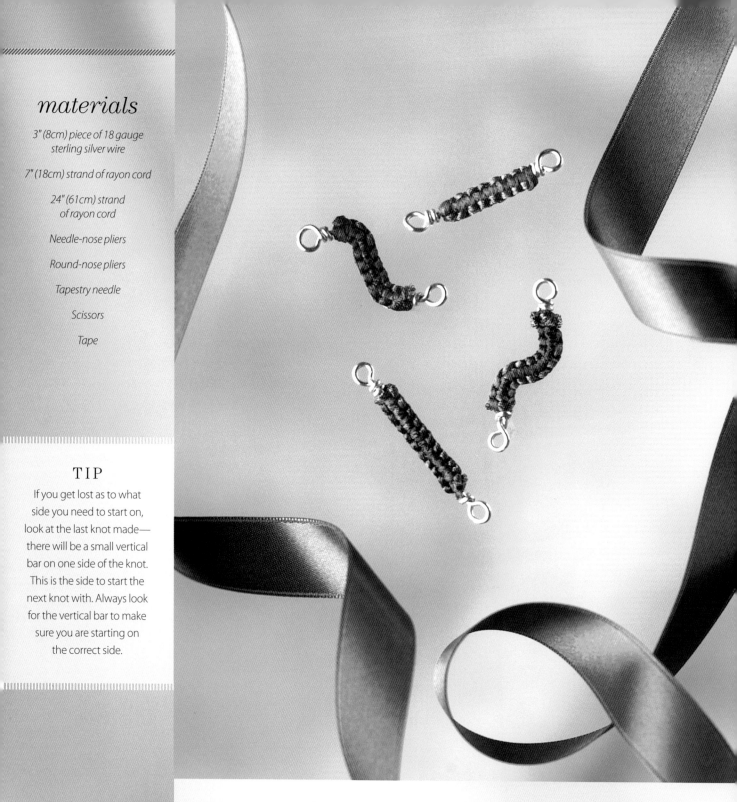

materials

3" (8cm) piece of 18 gauge
sterling silver wire

7" (18cm) strand of rayon cord

24" (61cm) strand
of rayon cord

Needle-nose pliers

Round-nose pliers

Tapestry needle

Scissors

Tape

TIP

If you get lost as to what
side you need to start on,
look at the last knot made—
there will be a small vertical
bar on one side of the knot.
This is the side to start the
next knot with. Always look
for the vertical bar to make
sure you are starting on
the correct side.

Square Knot Bead

*As much as I love the twist created with half-square knots, I also love the
neat and organized look of a square knot. I choose a fun variegated cord to
add some excitement to the finished bead.*

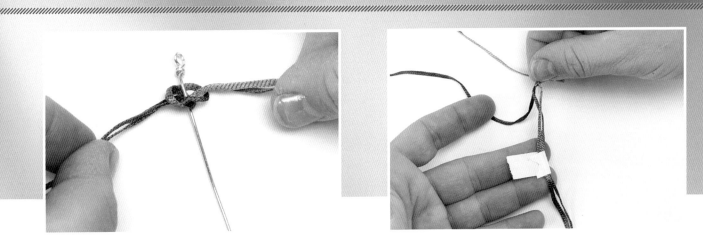

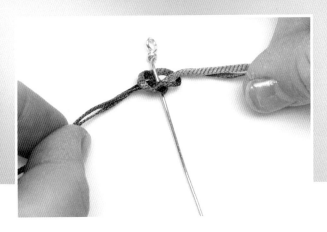

1 Prepare to begin

Create a wire-wrapped loop at the end of the 3" (8cm) piece of wire (see *Wire Wrapping*, page 23). Fold the 2 pieces of cord in half together. Tie the 2 pieces of cord to the wire using an overhand knot (see *Tying an Overhand Knot*, page 25).

2 Secure ends

Tape the 2 short tails to the bottom of the wire so they are taut. This will keep them in place as you work.

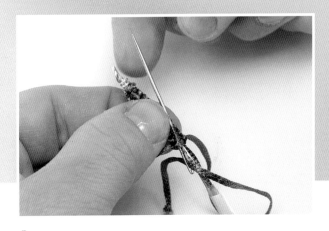

3 Begin knotting

To make a square knot, separate the 2 long pieces of cord with the wire in the middle. Take the cord on the left side and pull it to the right over the wire and under the right cord. Take the right cord under the left cord and behind the wire, pulling it to the left, then up through the loop on the left of the wire. Pull the knot snug around the wire to make the first half of the knot (half-square knot).

To make the second half of the square knot, take the cord on the right side and pull it to the left over the wire and under the left cord. Take the left cord under the right cord and behind the wire, pulling it to the right, then up through the loop on the right of the wire. Pull the knot snug around the wire to make the second half of the knot.

4 Finish bead

Repeat Step 3 to make square knots to cover about 1" (3cm) of the wire. Sew in the tails of the 2 longer pieces of cord (see *Sewing in Tails*, page 28). Untape the 2 short pieces of cord and trim them flush with the bottom square knot.

To complete the bead, make a second wire-wrapped loop at the open end of the wire.

materials

13 square knot beads

14 6mm jump rings

Lobster claw clasp

Needle-nose pliers

Round-nose pliers

TIP
Use a necklace stand to help bend and shape the necklace. When finishing, it is easier than using your own neck.

Rainbow Connection Necklace

I wanted the beads to dance around the neckline in this piece, so I bent the beads into an S shape. You can create different looks by bending the wire in different shapes, or by creating a chain using the square knot. Use different cords, ribbons and fibers together for a totally new look. However, remember to test fibers to see if you like the way they feel against your skin before using the fiber in a piece of jewelry. An itchy piece of jewelry isn't one you'll often pick out of your jewelry box!

1 Prepare beads

Follow the instructions on pages 114–115 to make 13 square knot beads. Grasp a bead at the top and bottom loops. Gently push one end and pull the other end to bend the bead into an S shape. Repeat to make 12 S beads.

2 Begin connections

Bend the remaining square knot bead into an arch for the center bead. Lay out the beads in the desired order with 6 S beads on each side of the arch bead. Open each jump ring (see *Opening and Closing Jump Rings*, page 22). Use a jump ring to connect 2 beads. Repeat to assemble the necklace.

3 Complete necklace

Use the last jump ring to attach the lobster claw clasp to the end of the necklace. Connect a jump ring to the opposite end to serve as the other half of the clasp.

CHAPTER EIGHT

Gallery

In this gallery are additional pieces of jewelry I made using the techniques in this book. I hope that they inspire you and start your creative juices flowing. I have listed a description with each piece along with the techniques I used from the book to create the piece. I have used one or two techniques in each piece to complement the projects in the book. Try combining beads using different techniques in one piece of jewelry or create a fiber chain to string the fabric beads on. The possibilities are endless with the basics in this book and a little imagination.

Once you have explored the techniques in this book, try mixing other jewelry techniques or sewing techniques to create your own beads and jewelry.

I hope that the projects throughout the book help you create your own stunning jewelry wardrobe. There is just nothing like receiving compliments on a piece of jewelry you are wearing that you have made.

Vintage Paisley

I created these paisley beads by cutting heavy-weight stabilizer into the desired shapes, covering them with a batik fabric and using the Bead Sandwich technique from Chapter 5. I mixed my paisley sandwich beads with vintage gold knot beads and an antique locket.

119

Eye of the Tiger

I created these octagon fabric beads using the Fabric Tile Beads technique from Chapter 5 with a rich brown print. I used a beautiful piece of tiger's eye as the focus piece for the necklace. Once the necklace was sewn together I coated the fabric beads with Clear Tar Gel for a lacquered wood look.

Crescent Moon

These Fabric Sculpted Beads from Chapter 4 were created with assorted cotton lamés. The fabric is wrapped around heavy-weight stabilizer cut into crescent moon and marquee shapes. The seed beads are sewn between the fabric beads to complete the necklace.

Essence of Asia

This is a simple and elegant example of the Fabric Barrel Beads shown in Chapter 3. I varied the width and the length of the fabric strips to create beads of different sizes for the necklace. The center bead is a handblown glass bead from Italy.

Roses and Scrolls

This piece uses Fabric Barrel Beads on Wire from Chapter 3. I bent the silver wire into an S shape before rolling the beads. Once I finished bending the wire, I wrapped this wonderful gold scroll fabric to finish the bead.

Blue Wave

I made these Square Knot Beads from Chapter 7 using variegated wool yarn. I bent each bead into a wave. Simple silver accent beads and silver beading wire accent the knotted beads. This necklace is simple and lightweight.

Ocean Elegance

This necklace shows the Fabric Bicone Beads from Chapter 3. I used a batik fabric that had a large range of cool colors across the fabric. The iridescent accent beads matched the fabric perfectly to create a calm underwater feel to the necklace.

Into the Forest

I created this necklace using a Triple Braided Chain. This chain is like the Double Braided Chain in Chapter 7, but two of the three strands are braided instead of just one. Though I rarely work with orange and green, this is one of my favorite pieces to wear.

Woodland Splendor

For this piece I created Layered Wool Beads like those in Chapter 6, but I shaped them to look like leaves. I used metallic paint to create the accent vines on the leaves. The focus bead is a copper-covered leaf and the accent beads are dyed fresh water pearls.

Platinum Garden

I used a silver batik fabric and silver eyelets for these Fabric Tile Beads with Eyelets from Chapter 5. To make the necklace I used flower connector beads and sterling silver jump rings to connect all the beads together. The necklace was finished with tiny bee beads for some added whimsy.

Dragonfly Dance

This piece was made by creating a simple chain from vintage hand-dyed cord. The pendant is a pewter charm I found at an antique store. The simplicity of the chain and charm make this another of my favorites to wear.

Raspberries and Cream

This necklace was created using wool roving beads from Chapter 6. I mixed vintage glass beads with the wool beads to complete the piece and used a porcelain pendant as the focus.

Five Moons

This necklace features the Thread Wrapped Washer technique from Chapter 4. The beads are made with rayon floss and assorted metal washers. This piece has a very delicate, expensive look to it, which is amazing since it is made from hardware and floss.

Resources

Here is a list of the supplies I used for many of the pieces in this book. Many of the products used in the book can be found at art stores, quilting stores and bead stores. I also suggest checking out antique stores and flea markets for old pieces of jewelry that can be cut apart to salvage the components. If you have any questions on any of the supplies and components I used in the book, please feel free to contact me at The Whimsical Workshop.

The Whimsical Workshop LLC.
1050 E. Ray Rd., A5-166
Chandler, AZ 85225
(888) 499-5715
www.TheWhimsicalWorkshop.com

Blank Quilting
www.blankquilting.com
Fabric

Bird Brain Designs
www.birdbraindesigns.com
Wool roving

Woolylady
www.woolylady.com
Wool fabric

Artgirlz
www.artgirlz.com
Wool roving, felt balls and accent pieces

Dill Buttons
www.dill-buttons.com
Buttons

Sonoran Beads
www.sonoranbeads.com
Glass beads

Nifty Thrifty Dry Goods
www.niftythriftydrygoods.com
Trims and cords

Presencia Hilaturas USA, Inc.
www.presenciausa.com
Threads

Rainbow Gallery
www.rainbowgallery.com
Rayon floss

Index

Explore new craft horizons
with these other fine F+W Media books.

Serge & Merge Quilts

Sharon V. Rotz with Nancy Zieman

Serging meets quilting in this project-driven title in the Create with Nancy series. Author Sharon Rotz uses serging stitches to create and embellish fifteen quilt projects in a range of styles and sizes, including bed quilts. Learn how to use a serger to do things for quilts that other machines can't.

paperback / 8.25" × 10.875" / 128 pages

ISBN-10: 0-89689-810-5 / ISBN-13: 978-0-89689-810-3 / SRN: Z2917

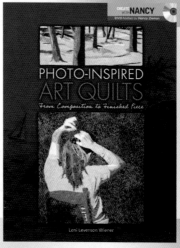

Photo-Inspired Art Quilts

From Composition to Finished Piece

Leni Levenson Wiener with Nancy Zieman

This title in the Create with Nancy series begins with instructions on how to select a photo for an art quilt, then shows how to translate that photo into a fabric collage that can be accented and embellished with thread painting and raw-edge appliqué. Fifteen exercises outline different skills and artistic concepts needed to create art quilts from photography.

paperback / 8.25" × 10.875" / 128 pages

ISBN-10: 0-89689-804-0 / ISBN-13: 978-0-89689-804-2 / SRN: Z2873

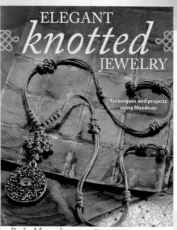

Elegant Knotted Jewelry

Techniques and Projects Using Maedeup

Becky Meverden

Explore the wonderful world of maedeup knotting, a Korean knotting art. Becky Meverden first shows ten basic maedeup knots, then uses those knots in thirty upscale jewelry projects, including bracelets, necklaces, earrings and more.

paperback / 8.25" × 10.875" / 128 pages

ISBN-10: 0-89689-818-0 / ISBN-13: 978-0-89689-818-9 / SRN: Z2955

These and other fine Krause Publications titles are available at your local craft retailer, bookstore or online supplier, or visit our Web site at www.mycraftivitystore.com.